Speaking Frames: How t for Writing: Ages 8–10

Now in a new format, *Speaking Frames: How to Teach Talk for Writing: Ages 8–10* brings together material from Sue Palmer's popular Speaking Frames books for primary classes. Providing an innovative and effective answer to the problem of teaching speaking and listening, this book offers a range of speaking frames for children to 'fill in' orally, developing their language patterns and creativity, and boosting their confidence in talk for learning and talk for writing. Fully updated, this book offers:

- material for individual, paired and group presentations;
- links to cross-curricular 'skeletons';
- support notes for teachers and assessment guidance;
- advice on flexible progression and working to a child's ability;
- suggestions for developing individual pupils' spoken language skills.

With a wealth of photocopiable sheets and creative ideas for speaking and listening, *Speaking Frames: How to Teach Talk for Writing: Ages 8–10* is essential reading for all practising, trainee and recently qualified teachers who wish to develop effective speaking and listening in their classroom.

Sue Palmer is a writer, broadcaster and education consultant. Specialising in the teaching of literacy, she has authored over 150 books and has contributed to numerous television programmes and software packages. She is the author of *How to Teach Writing Across the Curriculum: Ages 6–8* and *How to Teach Writing Across the Curriculum: Ages 8–14*, also published by Routledge.

Also available:

Speaking Frames: How to Teach Talk for Writing: Ages 10–14
Sue Palmer
(ISBN: 978-0-415-57987-2)

Speaking Frames: How to Teach Talk for Writing: Ages 8–10

Sue Palmer

Routledge
Taylor & Francis Group

LONDON AND NEW YORK

This first edition published 2011
by Routledge
2 Park Square, Milton Park, Abingdon, Oxon, OX14 4RN

Simultaneously published in the USA and Canada
by Routledge
270 Madison Avenue, New York, NY 10016

Routledge is an imprint of the Taylor & Francis Group, an informa business

Typeset in Helvetica by FiSH Books, Enfield
Printed and bound in Great Britain by the MPG Books Group

British Library Cataloguing in Publication Data
A catalogue record for this book is available from the British Library

Library of Congress Cataloging-in-Publication Data
Palmer, Sue.
  Speaking frames : how to teach talk for writing, ages 8–10 / By Sue Palmer. — 1st ed.
    p. cm.
  1. Oral communication—Study and teaching. 2. Discourse analysis—Study and teaching. 3. Written communication—Study and teaching. 4. Rhetoric—Study and teaching. I. Title.
  P95.3.P35 2011
  372.62—dc22

ISBN13: 978-0-415-57982-7 (pbk)
ISBN13: 978-0-203-84613-1 (ebk)

Contents

Introducing speaking frames

Speaking frames are frameworks for directed speaking and listening activities in the primary classroom. They are specifically designed to help pupils move on from the restricted patterns of spoken language to the more complex patterns of written language and 'literate talk'. In this way, it is hoped they will help develop children's control over language in both speaking and writing.

Spoken and written language patterns

It is now well established that written language is very different from the spoken variety. Speech is generally interactive – we bat words and phrases back and forth – and produced within a shared context, so it's fragmented, disorganised and a great deal of meaning goes by on the nod. In fact, you can get by in speech without ever forming a sentence, or at least only very simple ones. To make links between ideas, speakers tend to use very simple connectives, like the ubiquitous *and* or, to denote sequence, *and then.* This kind of language is described by linguists as 'spontaneous speech'.

On the other hand, written language is produced for an unknown, unseen audience, who may have no background knowledge at all about the subject. It must therefore be explicit and carefully crafted. It requires more extensive vocabulary than speech and organisation into sentences for clarity. The sentences become increasingly complex as the writer expresses increasingly complex ideas, using a widening range of connectives to show how these ideas relate to each other.

The interface between speech and writing

The more 'literate' someone is, the more written language patterns also begin to inform their speech. Exposure to literate language through reading, and the opportunity to develop control of it oneself through writing, leads to increasingly literate spoken language. It seems to be a cyclical process: speech informs writing, which then informs speech, which informs writing, and so on. In general, the more accomplished the writer, the better equipped he or she is to 'talk like a book'.

Until the late nineteenth century, this interface between speech and writing was universally acknowledged. From the time of the ancient Greeks, **rhetoric** (reading aloud, speaking persuasively) was considered as essential a part of education as reading and writing – perhaps even more so. Exercises in rhetoric were intended to develop not only pupils' powers of oratory, but also their ear for language – the explicit, complex patterns of language in which educated people converse and write. As Ben Jonson put it in 1640:

For a man to write well, there are required three necessaries: to read the best authors, to hear the best speakers, and much exercise of his own style.

However, the introduction of universal state education automatically meant large classes in which speech for the many was not deemed possible (or desirable), and the literacy curriculum was restricted to reading and writing. Throughout the twentieth century, educators have concentrated their attention on literacy at the expense of oracy. Speaking frames provide a twenty-first century approach to the forgotten 'fourth R'.

The 'two horses' model

Speaking frames were initially developed as an aid to writing. Teaching children to write without first giving opportunities to speak is, fairly obviously, 'putting the cart before the horse'. However, opportunities for talk before writing do not necessarily develop literate language patterns. Ideally, there should be two 'oracy horses' drawing the 'writing cart'.

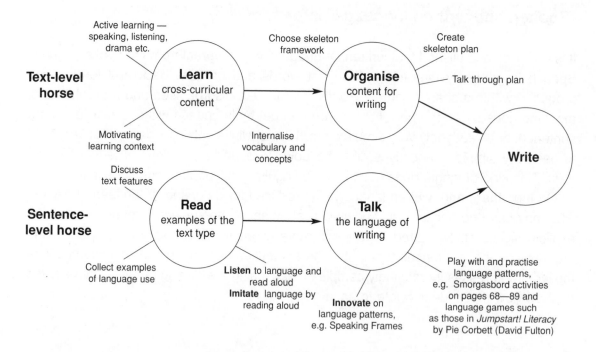

Figure 1 Two horses before the cart model

The first 'horse' works at text level – it's 'talk for learning'. These spoken language activities are vital for helping children to:

- engage with the subject under discussion;
- familiarise themselves with key vocabulary;
- get to grips with underlying concepts;
- organise their ideas appropriately before they write.

The talk will generally be interactive, context-dependent and conducted in the language of spontaneous speech. There are many suggestions for providing 'talk for learning' in *How to Teach Writing Across the Curriculum: Ages 8–14* (Routledge, 2011).

The second is a sentence level horse – 'talk for writing'. This is the opportunity for children to develop knowledge about and familiarity with the sorts of language appropriate to writing. Speaking frames were developed as a means of focusing on elements of literate language in which to express ideas clearly and coherently for an unknown audience.

Listen – Imitate – Innovate – Invent

There is a well established developmental model for the way children acquire speech: first they **listen** to adult speakers and **imitate** elements of their speech; they then begin to **innovate** on these language patterns; finally they use all this language data to **invent** their own expressions. However, in terms of acquiring written language patterns – which are, indeed, much more demanding in terms of form and complexity – we make little provision for the first three stages. All too often, we ask children to go straight to invention.

For children with a strong background of literacy this may not be a problem. If they come from families where 'literate talk' is the norm, they may well absorb and reproduce many of its features as naturally as we all acquire spontaneous speech patterns. There is another group of children who are likely to absorb written language patterns without effort, whatever their social background. These are the ones who learn to read easily, and who then become committed readers, tackling a wide range of reading matter. They'll pick up written language patterns through frequent exposure to the printed page. However, in a multimedia world, where children can access all the entertainment and information they want via visual displays on a screen, fewer and fewer of them are reading widely in their leisure time. For the majority of children, unless we provide structured help, learning to write will be inhibited by a lack of appropriate vocabulary, language constructions and cohesive devices.

Integrating 'Listen – Imitate – Innovate – Invent' into teaching

Many teachers now spend time before children write familiarising them with key aspects of a particular text type – building up a 'writer's toolkit' of organisational and linguistic features. Many of these language patterns are unfamiliar to children, so opportunities to listen, imitate and innovate can develop familiarity and help children internalise linguistic features, making them available both for writing and for literate talk.

- **Listen**: children need opportunities to *hear* literate language as often as possible, to become familiar with the rhythms and patterns of sentences, and of specific phrases and constructions particularly useful for a text type.
- **Imitate**: they also need the chance to produce literate language patterns from their own mouths – to know how more sophisticated vocabulary and phraseology *feels*, and to respond physically to the ebb and flow of well-constructed sentences.
- **Innovate**: then they need opportunities to innovate on those patterns, expressing their own ideas and understanding through the medium of literate talk.

One way of ensuring children **listen** to and **imitate** written language patterns is through reading aloud to them and ensuring they have plenty of opportunities to read aloud themselves (paired reading with a partner – one paragraph each – is a good way of ensuring the latter). However, it is difficult to target specific language patterns in this way, and reading aloud does not provide an opportunity to **innovate**.

Figure 2 The patterns of written language

How speaking frames work

Speaking frames replicate the listen – imitate – innovate model for specific types of language as part of children's learning across the curriculum. In pairs, groups or as individuals, pupils work on a specific task and fit their answers into a given frame for oral presentation to the class. The class therefore **listens** to a number of presentations based on the frame:

- first by the teacher, as he or she demonstrates the process;
- next by more able pupils, selected by the teacher as likely to provide good and fluent models;
- then by their remaining peers.

And every child has an opportunity to **imitate** and **innovate** on the same language patterns as they make their own presentation.

Nine specific speaking frames are provided, as a starting point for teachers and pupils. There is also a 'smorgasbord' of useful sentence starts relating to the sorts of talking and writing children need in Year 4. Teachers can use these as they are (see the notes with each photocopiable page) and/or take from them to make further speaking frames based on the cross-curricular work or literacy objectives being pursued by the class.

The importance of literate talk

Although speaking frames were originally devised to help children get to grips with written language, their potential for the development of children's oral language skills is probably even more important. The frames facilitate the virtuous circle described above of 'speech informs writing . . . informs speech . . . informs writing . . . informs speech . . .', and thus should help develop children's powers of literate speech as much they develop written work. The sooner we can help make children familiar and comfortable with the patterns of literate talk the better. As Thomas Jefferson put it:

Style, in writing or speaking, is formed very early in life, when the imagination is warm and impressions are permanent.

Many children find speaking in front of an audience difficult, often because they do not have access to patterns of literate talk. Trapped in spontaneous spoken language patterns, their vocabulary is limited and speech is fragmented, incoherent and lacking in organisation. Speaking frames provide support in translating their ideas into coherent sentences; preparing their presentation gives the time to consider vocabulary, develop explicitness and experiment with more formal connectives than they would usually use. Practice makes perfect, and the opportunities provided here to practise presentation skills should also develop children's confidence, social skills and self-esteem.

In the modern world, there's another hugely important reason for developing powers of literate talk. As the use of voice-activated software proliferates in the workplace, 'writers' of the future may seldom actually *write* very much at all. They'll be expected to compose and dictate texts directly into machines. This requires excellent command of spoken language – so 'talk for writing' may in the long run be more important than writing itself.

The 'two horses' model for teaching was developed with this probability in mind. It therefore prepares pupils to learn, organise and record their understanding at text level, then 'talk it into print' at sentence level – for further information on this process see the Appendix on pages 90–96 and *How to Teach Writing Across the Curriculum: Ages 8–14* (Routledge, 2011). While the physical act of writing is essential as children acquire literacy skills, in their adult lives the successful production of text is likely to depend far more on their capacity for literate talk.

A note on assessment

The speaking frames provided are for three types of presentation: children working in pairs, as individuals and in groups of around six. Each type of presentation requires preliminary teaching, which can be covered using the three sample frames.

However, speaking and listening are notoriously difficult to assess, and this is particularly the case with 'talk for writing', where many social, intellectual and linguistic sub-skills are brought together in reaching the final presentation. This book breaks the pupil's performance into four elements, covered in two teaching sections:

- Section 1: Introducing the activity;
  - **preparation** for the presentation
  - the **content** of the presentation.
- Section 2: Staging the presentation;
  - specific **language** use in the presentation (moving towards literate language)
  - **presentation** skills.

Because so many skills are involved, it is difficult to be precise about teaching objectives. Teachers should of course concentrate on objectives as appropriate to the ability and experience of pupils.

However, too much emphasis on specific objectives here could lead to very reductionist teaching. The activities cover many aspects of the literacy curriculum as well as cross-curricular thinking skills, social skills and the development of self-esteem. The true learning objective is the orchestration of all these skills in pursuit of a clearly defined outcome: the presentation itself. While the teacher may choose to emphasise a particular aspect of any of the four elements listed above, it should always be seen within the context of the whole activity.

Simple assessment sheets are provided for each of the types of presentation, to help teachers focus on the performance of specific children, pairs or groups. Another means of assessment is to video or audiotape children's presentations and let them assess their own performance using the *Giving the Talk* sheet as a checklist.

Paired presentations

Paired presentations are the easiest type of speaking frame presentation. Children who have previously used a 'talking partners' technique should adjust to using frames quickly; for those who have not used the technique, the frames are an ideal introduction.

Preparatory materials

Stage 1: We're thinking of . . .

In the three *We're thinking of . . .* exercises, children develop and present a short presentation, using literate language patterns, with the support of a partner. The 'quiz' aspect of the talks provides motivation for explicit description of the objects, animals and places concerned.

The three talks are designed to introduce children to the sound of formal 'literate language' issuing from their own mouths, and to develop their control of explicit language. Children often feel explicit language involves 'stating the obvious', but such explicitness is essential for the understanding and communication of ideas:

- **Task 1: *We're thinking of something*** involves working together to analyse and describe the characteristics of a familiar object with as great a degree of explicitness as possible (scientific thinking).
- **Task 2: *We're thinking of an animal*** involves collaborative research, analysis and description of the characteristics of an animal (scientific thinking).
- **Task 3**: ***We're thinking of somewhere*** involves paired discussion to imagine the characteristics of a setting (known or imagined), using all the senses (imaginative thinking).

Stage 2: Check it out

In the three *Check it out* activities, pairs of children develop and present a series of short presentations about a piece of research undertaken together. The frames provide a structured route through essential library and research skills, so teachers can use these tasks as a vehicle for developing skills (which should be taught to the class before the paired task is given). Brief notes are provided opposite each frame.

The three talks are designed to help children report on their work in more formal 'literate language' than they would usually use. This gives them to chance to speak in these literate patterns prior to using them in written work, and to develop their control of technical vocabulary related to research skills.

- **Task 1: *Planning research*** involves working together to choose an area of research, thinking clearly about what they know, what they need to know, and how they can find it out, then reporting to the class on what they have done.
- **Task 2: *A non-fiction book*** involves appraising a non-fiction book for its contents and usefulness in this research, and explaining their findings using the technical terminology associated with non-fiction reading.
- **Task 3: *Paragraphs and keywords*** involves collaborative work analysing a sequence of paragraphs are in a non-fiction book, identifying the gist of each paragraph and the keywords to sum it up, and commenting on the organisation of the piece as a whole.

The frames specifically cover these aspects of literate talk:

- speaking in complete sentences;
- varying sentence construction;
- the importance of explicitness;
- the standard English '... and I' (as opposed to 'Me and ...');
- the use of descriptive and technical vocabulary;
- the language of exemplification (*such as, for instance, for example*);
- terminology associated with non-fiction reading (e.g.*index, scan*);
- 'literate' connectives (e.g. *however, also, on the whole*).

GETTING READY

1. Read the frame and talk about the presentation with your partner. Work out how you are going to do it.

2. Read each section of the frame. Talk about the best way to finish it. Jot down keywords to remind you.

3. Go back and check it through. Have you chosen the best words? Is there anything you need to change or add? (You can add extra sentences if you want.)

4. Practise your presentation together, taking turns to say one section each. Read the words of the frame, then finish the section in your own words.

5. Listen to each other and make improvements. Practise till you can do it easily.

Introducing paired presentations

Children need training in order to work productively in pairs. When you first start paired talk it is best to select the pairs yourself, choosing children you know will work well together. As children get used to the technique, they should be able to work with whoever happens to be sitting next to them.

- Display enlarged copies of the *Getting Ready* notes and the relevant speaking frame.
- Read the frame with pupils. Explain that it is a sort of quiz – as each pair reports back the rest of the class will listen carefully and try to guess what they're thinking of.
- Go through the *Getting Ready* notes, and demonstrate each stage, working with a partner – another adult or an able child. Model the sorts of behaviour and outcome you are looking for, as in the 'points to watch for' boxes below.
- Give out small copies of the frame for pupils to work with.

Give the pairs an appropriate amount of time to decide exactly what they are going to say, and to rehearse it. Then watch how the pairs are interacting, and make sure they know you're watching. Tell them you won't necessarily intervene if things are not going well: they have to learn to work cooperatively, and can't always rely on you to sort out problems. You could use the assessment sheet on page 23 to focus on the work of some pairs.

Points to watch for during preparation

Collaboration	Are they sharing tasks and ideas? Is one partner dominating?
Reflecting on content	Are they taking time talking through each section?
Refining ideas	Do their ideas develop, change, improve through discussion?
Note-making	Do notes cover keywords for the presentation? Are both partners involved in making notes?
Practice	Do they practise? Do they use practice to improve content and presentation? Do they give useful feedback to each other?

Points to watch for in content

Choice of topic	Is it a mutual choice? Is it suitable/interesting? Is it easily guessable?
Accuracy	Are their statements/descriptions factually accurate? If necessary, are they able to find out information?
Effectiveness	Are they providing the bare minimum response or looking for more engaging detail and means of expression?
keywords	Are they choosing good keywords – precise nouns, suitable adjectives, good choice of verbs?

Don't interrupt pupils who are going well. Where you decide intervention is necessary, use questioning strategies to help them on course:

- *What's the problem here?*
- *If you don't agree, how can you find a solution?*
- *Where could you go to find a good word?*

Give positive feedback about the discussions at the end of the session, e.g.:

- *I liked the way Andrew and Asif shared their ideas.*
- *I liked the quiet voices these pairs used, so they wouldn't disturb others.*
- *I thought Maria and Shara were very clever to go and use the thesaurus.*
- *I like Jan and Simon's notes – when they've fed back to the class we must have a look at those.*

Then move straight into presentation – see next page.

GIVING THE TALK

1. Make sure you know who is going to say each section so you can switch back and forward without fuss.

2. When you are presenting, think about your audience – not yourself or your partner.

- Are you speaking slowly enough for everyone to follow what you say?
- Is your voice loud enough to hear?
- Are you looking at the audience?
- Are you doing anything that will distract them (like giggling, wriggling or fiddling with your paper)?

---

3. If anything goes wrong, try to put it right without fuss. Help your partner and let your partner help you.

Staging paired presentations

Choose a few pairs of children who are ready and ask them to present their talks while the class listens attentively and guesses.

- Display an enlarged copy of the *Giving The Talk* notes opposite, and talk through them with pupils, drawing attention to the key points in the box.
- For *We're Thinking of...* arrange an unobtrusive signal, such as folding their arms, by which the rest of the class can quietly indicate when they guess the answer.

Points to watch for in language

Sentence structure	Do they use the frame to speak in sentences? Does their expression indicate awareness of sentence boundaries? Are any extra sentences framed correctly?
Explicitness	Is the language clear, explicit, evocative? How much detail have they added?
Vocabulary	Is vocabulary varied or repetitive? Have they used precise nouns, suitable adjectives and verbs?
Standard English	Have they used the vocabulary and grammar of standard English?

Points to watch for in presentation

Turn-taking/ collaboration	Is their turn-taking organised or chaotic? Do they work together or as two individuals? If necessary, do they help each other out?
Pace	Is delivery of each speaker too fast or too slow?
Voice	Is each speaker audible? Are voices expressive or monotonous?
Audience engagement	Do they address the audience or each other?
Body language	Do they stand confidently or self-consciously? Do they use gesture to enhance speech? Do they wriggle or fuss with their notes?
Dealing with problems	Are they easily distracted? If anything goes wrong do they deal with it satisfactorily?

Give brief feedback to the pair on key points of their performance. Give specific praise wherever possible, e.g.:

- *I really liked your description because it had lots of detail and interesting words.*
- *You used the speaking frame very well, and your talk was all in good clear sentences.*
- *I loved the way you took turns, with each person's speech flowing on from the other's.*

Where feedback is negative, give it from the point of view of the audience, e.g.:

- *Sometimes it was difficult to hear because you were speaking very quickly.*
- *You have such a quiet voice we couldn't hear everything you said.*
- *I'm afraid I was distracted by the way you were fiddling with the book.*

If you invite the rest of the class to comment on aspects of the performance (perhaps basing it on the *Giving The Talk* notes), ensure the criticism is constructive. As pupils become more experienced at giving paired presentations, feedback can become more detailed and specific.

If each presentation and feedback takes about five to eight minutes, you should be able to hear about six pairs while still maintaining the interest of the class. Some pairs may also need more time to prepare. Provide further time as necessary, then give opportunities for all the pairs to present their talks, probably about six at a time. Each time, begin by revising the *Giving The Talk* notes and reminding children of what they have learned from other pairs. Some pairs may wish to repeat their presentations in the light of what they learn – this should be encouraged.

■ We're thinking of

A MAN-MADE OBJECT

_____ and I are thinking of a man-made object that is about as big as _____ .

It is _____
_____ .

When you touch/hold this object it feels
_____ .

It is made of _____
_____ .

You would probably find it in _____
_____ .

It is used for _____
_____ .

'**Emma** and I are thinking of a man-made object that is about as big as **a cupboard**.

It is **usually shaped like a cube and is mostly black in colour with a grey screen on the front and wires at the back**.

When you touch this object it feels **hard and smooth. If it is switched off it is cold, but when it is switched on it feels slightly warm.**

It is made of **metal, glass and plastic with electronic parts inside**.

You would probably find it in **the living room or bedroom of someone's house**.

It is used for **showing programmes. People watch them for fun or to find out about the world**.'

Talk about:

● The meaning of 'man-made'. Discuss the many possible items to choose, e.g.:

pieces of furniture	toys or sporting equipment
types of transport	items of clothing
tools or utensils	familiar machines

It helps to give time for children to choose – perhaps outlining the task before break or lunchtime, so pairs can think about it together beforehand.

● Being sure you know exactly what your object looks like, is made of, etc..
Thinking of something to compare in size, e.g.:

a mountain	an elephant
a car	a table
a shoebox	a spoon
a fingernail	an ant

● How to deal with 'touch/hold'. Show children how to decide which is most appropriate to the item they are describing, and to delete the alternative word.

● Taking time to build up your description. This involves using your imagination and thinking around the item.

● Keep on improving on your description as you practice.

● Trying to use 'grown-up' language structures and vocabulary, e.g.:

'shaped like a cuboid'	'black in colour'

■ We're thinking of

AN ANIMAL

_____ and I are thinking of an animal which is about the size of a _____ .

This animal is _____ in colour,
_____ .

It has _____ legs and its body is covered in
_____ .

It also has _____
_____ .

The animal's habitat is _____
_____ .

This animal eats _____
_____ .

'**Asif** and I are thinking of an animal which is about the size of **a Labrador dog**.

This animal is **mostly black** in colour, **with white stripes on its face and a white belly**.

It has **four** legs and its body is covered in **fur.**

It also has **strong front paws for digging and sharp teeth for tearing prey and defending its territory**.

The animal's habitat is **called a sett, and is underground. It builds its sett in quiet woodlands. You find it all over the British Isles and other parts of the world with the same type of climate**.

This animal eats **insects, grubs and small animals and birds. It also eats roots and shoots**.'

Talk about:

- Choosing an animal you can find out about easily. Ensure that there are plenty of useful reference books available. Choosing and researching an animal will take some time – it may be helpful to set this as homework.
- Checking to make sure your description is factually accurate.
- Taking time to build up your description. Add extra sentences to the frame if you have further information, but try to add it at the most suitable point.
  Keep on improving your description to make it clear, e.g.:

    'strong front paws for digging'

- Using 'grown-up' language constructions and vocabulary, e.g.:

    'tearing its prey'   'defending its territory'
    'the same type of climate'   'it also eats'

■ We're thinking of

SOMEWHERE

_____ and I are thinking of a place which is indoors/outdoors.

> If you were in this place you would probably be able to hear _____
> _____ .

You might be feeling _____ .

> In this place you might be able to smell _____
> _____ .

You would probably see _____
_____ .

> We would/would not like to visit this place because
> _____
> _____ .

'**Brian** and I are thinking of a place which can be indoors or outdoors.

If you were in this place you would probably be able to hear **shouts, laughter and splashing.**

You might be feeling **wet and perhaps a bit shivery. Your feet would feel hard cold tiles beneath them. If it is outdoors, the way you feel would depend on the weather, but indoors it is usually quite warm.**

In this place you might be able to smell **a chemical called chlorine. You might also smell wet human bodies!**

You would probably see **people in swimming costumes, splashing about in clear blue water. Some of them might have rubber rings or lilos. You would also see diving boards, and perhaps water chutes and springboards. The whole place would probably be tiled and quite light in colour.**

We would like to visit this place because **we both like swimming and messing about in water.**

Talk about:

- Choosing a place. Provide some examples to get them thinking, e.g.:

kitchen	beach	funfair
classroom	countryside	football stadium
school hall	busy road	aircraft
supermarket	garden	bus

- How to deal with 'indoors/outdoors'. Show children how to decide which fits the place they are describing, and to delete the alternative word (or adjust as we have if necessary).
- Taking time to build up your description. This involves using your imagination and thinking yourself into the environment. The sentence frames encourage the use of all the senses.
- Keep on improving on your description as you practice.
- Trying to use 'grown-up' language structures and vocabulary, e.g.:

  'a chemical called chlorine'   'quite light in colour'

■ Check it out

PLANNING RESEARCH

_____ and I are researching _____ .

We already know that _____ .

We also know _____ .

However, we think we need to know more about
_____ .

It might also help to find out _____
_____ .

To find out more about our topic we are going to
start by _____ .

We could also try _____
_____ .

Before using this speaking frame, children should know how to approach a piece of research by brainstorming under the headings:

- What do we know?
- What do we need to know?
- How will we find out?

If this has been taught through class lessons, this paired activity is a useful follow-up task.

'**Hannah** and I are researching **Anne Frank**.

We already know that **she lived during the Second World War and had to hide from the Nazi soldiers**.

We also know **that she wrote a diary about it.**

However, we think we ought to know more about **how she and her family managed to hide and survive, who helped them and how long they were hidden.**

It might also help to find out **what happened in the end. We think she died but we don't know how or when.**

To find out more about our topic we are going to start by **looking in the school library for books about Anne Frank or the Second World War.**

We could also try **looking up Anne Frank on the internet, and in encyclopaedias.**'

Pairs of children could research

- topics related to cross-curricular work;
- topics of their choice.

Talk about:

- the research skills involved (see above);
- the ways in which the speaking frame avoids repetitive sentence structures (in reporting back something of this kind, most children would begin every sentence in the same way, e.g. *We found some ...*, *We scanned ...*, *We spotted ...*);
- the 'grown up' connectives, *However* and *also* (see pages 74–75).

■ Check it out

A NON-FICTION BOOK

_____ and I are researching _____ .

> We chose this book, called _____ .

It is by _____ and was published in _____ .

> In the Contents we found some useful chapter
> headings, such as _____ .

When we scanned through the book, we noticed other
items that might help. For instance, _____ .

> In the index we spotted some keywords that might
> be useful to us, including _____ .

Before using this speaking frame, children should know how to appraise the usefulness of a non-fiction book for their research by:

- scanning contents list, headings, captions, etc.;
- checking keywords in the index;
- checking the age of the book through the copyright date.

If all this has been taught through class lessons, this paired activity provides a useful follow-up task.

'**Mahinder** and I are researching **Anne Frank, who was a girl who wrote a diary about hiding from the Nazis in the Second World War.**

We chose this book called *Children in the Second World War.*

It is by **Kenna Bourke** and was published in **2003.**

In the Contents we found out some useful chapter headings such as **Anne Frank** and **Anne Frank's Diary.**

When we scanned through the book we noticed other items that might help. For instance **on page 7 there is a picture of Anne, with a caption that said 'Jews like Anne Frank were forced into hiding'. We kept an eye open for more about Jews and found something about Jewish children on page 33.**

In the index we spotted some keywords that might be useful to us, including **Anne Frank, Jews and Nazis. We also found some other places to look in the Bibliography, including Anne's diary and a good website.**'

Talk about:

- the research skills involved (see above);
- the 'technical language' associated with books, e.g. *copyright, index, contents, headings, captions*;
- the language used to introduce examples (*such as, For instance, including*);
- the use of the word *items.* This can be a useful substitute for the looser word *things* that children tend to use;
- using the book as a visual aid for the talk and perhaps pointing to relevant pages/features as they refer to them.

PARAGRAPHS AND KEYWORDS

_____ and I have been reading this passage about _____ . It consists of _____ paragraphs.

It is from a book called _____ by _____ and was published in _____ .

The first paragraph is _____ . Some of the keywords are _____ .

The next/third/fourth paragraph is about _____ . Keywords here include _____ .

The final paragraph is _____ .The keywords in this paragraph are _____ .

We think the author organised these paragraphs like this because _____ .

Before using this speaking frame, children should know how to analyse the organisation and content of a sequence of paragraphs in a non-fiction book:

- read the passage through to get an overview;
- highlight or underline keywords in each paragraph;
- summarise the content of the paragraph in a single sentence;
- work out how the paragraphs reflect the underlying structure of the text, which often relates to the text type, and may be illustrated diagrammatically, e.g.:

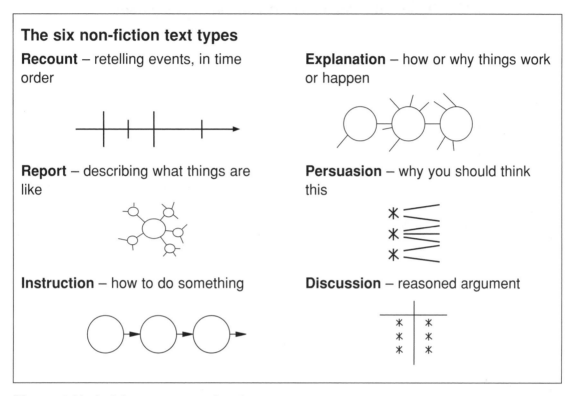

Figure 3 Underlying structures for six text types

'**Hannah** and I have been reading this passage about **Anne Frank.** It consists of **three** paragraphs and a short picture story.

The first paragraph is **an introduction about how Hitler treated Jewish people and how some people helped them. Some** of the keywords are *Hitler, Jewish people, dangerous, imprisoned, murdered, families, tried to help, punished or killed, a million and a half Jewish children died.*

The next paragraph is about **how some Jewish families hid in Holland and other countries, and how hard their lives were.** Keywords here include *constant danger, lived in secret, never went out, relying on other people.*

The third paragraph **summarises what happened to Anne Frank.** Some keywords are *famous, Holland, Holocaust, family and four others, two years, rooms above office, Amsterdam.*

The final **part of the passage is a picture story with captions telling about Anne's life.** The keywords are *1933 aged 4, Amsterdam; school, new friends;*

> **1940 Hitler invaded Holland; 1942 hiding, rooms above office; 1944 Nazi police-men, sent to prison, concentration camp, died of typhus.**
>
> We think the author organised the paragraphs like this because **she started with a wide view and narrowed down to focus on Anne. She started with the dangers to <u>all</u> Jewish children in Hitler's time, then she talked about those who went into hiding in places like Holland, next she set the scene about Anne and finally the picture story gave the details of Anne's life. It was like in a film where you see the big picture first and then it narrows in to one person.'**

Talk about:

- how you really need to display the text you have analysed (perhaps on an OHT or in an enlarged form);
- how to choose keywords (words and phrases that sum up the content);
- looking for the structure underlying the paragraphing, and perhaps representing it diagrammatically, e.g. the structure described in the example might be represented thus:

Assessment sheet

Paired presentation

Names _____ Date _____

_____

Preparation	Presentation
collaboration	*turn-taking and collaboration*
reflecting on content	*pace, volume, expression*
refining ideas	*engagement with audience*
note-making	*body language*
practice	*dealing with distractions/problems*
Content	**Language**
choice of topic	*sentence completion and organisation*
research skills	*explicitness*
effectiveness	*vocabulary*
keywords	*standard English*

Suggestions for the types of behaviour to watch for are given on pages 5 and 8.

Individual presentations

These activities provide opportunities for children to give a short sustained talk on their own. We suggest using the paired activities first, to familiarise children with (a) the use of the frames and (b) speaking out to the class, because for many, delivering a talk alone is a daunting task.

Preparatory material

Stage 1: Show and tell

Having an item of some sort to show to the class draws attention away from the speaker to some extent – as well as helping to illustrate the speech (thus supplementing language as a source of information).

These activities are designed to develop control of explicit language, this time without the aid of preliminary discussion, or the 'quiz' aspect on the paired task. Children have to learn how to put themselves in the position of an audience which has no prior knowledge about the item they are describing or explaining. The three *Show and Tells* gradually build up the level of language control required:

- **Personal treasure**: involves talking clearly about something personally well-known to the speaker, explaining and justifying the choice.
- **A natural object**: involves researching, thinking and talking about the characteristics of familiar item (scientific thinking).
- **A tool or utensil**: involves researching, thinking and talking about the characteristics of a familiar item, and explaining a simple process (scientific and technological thinking).

These frames specifically cover these aspects of literate talk:

- speaking in complete sentences;
- varying sentence construction;
- the importance of explicitness;
- key questions to answer (who, what, when, where, why);
- significant, descriptive and technical vocabulary;
- changing from singular to plural.

Stage 2: My favourite…

The *My Favourite…* talks draw on the child's personal responses to literature and television, and provide opportunities for summary, recount and justifying opinion.

The three presentations gradually build up the level of critical appreciation and language control required:

- **My favourite book (fiction)**: involves summarising the plot of a book, describing a character and an appealing section of the book, and justifying value judgements.
- **My favourite TV programme**: involves researching details of the broadcast, summarising its content, justifying opinions about it and drawing attention to a particular feature.
- **My favourite poem**: involves choosing a poem, summarising its content, commenting on when it was written (and how you know), reciting a few favourite lines and commenting critically upon them.

These frames specifically cover these aspects of literate talk:

- speaking in complete sentences;
- varying language (*my favourite...; the part I like best*);
- precise use of language in summary;
- the language of argument/justifying opinion.

GETTING READY

1. Read the frame and choose your subject. Make sure you'll have plenty to say about it.

2. Read each section of the frame. Think how you'll finish it. Jot down keywords to remind you. Add extra sentences if you want to.

3. If it helps you sort out your thoughts, you could write the whole thing out. But you can't just read your presentation.

4. Check it through. Is there anything you need to change or add?

5. Practise your presentation. Get an audience if you can – they may be able to help you make it better. Practise until you can do it easily.

Introducing individual talks

For each activity, give children plenty of time to choose their topic and plan the talk in advance. This makes an ideal homework exercise, but ensure they are well-prepared in class beforehand:

- Display enlarged copies of the *Getting Ready* notes and the relevant speaking frame. Read and discuss the frame with pupils.
- Go through the *Getting Ready* notes and demonstrate each stage, modelling the sorts of behaviour and outcomes you want from the pupils (a completed frame is provided each time).
- When you come to practise the talk, get pupils to 'help' you by reading the sentence starts in chorus.
- Give out copies of the frame for pupils to work on.

Some children may want to compose and write out their entire talk. This is fine, but they should use the frame and notes to deliver the talk, not just read a 'prepared speech'.

Some children may want to write and memorise their talk. This is also fine, as it helps develop auditory memory, but they should retain the frame and notes as an aide memoir in case memory fails.

When observing pupils' preparation (or assessing/discussing their frames and notes before the talks), watch for the following areas. You could use the assessment sheet on page 44 to focus on the work of some children.

Points to watch for during preparation

Reflecting on content	Does s/he take time to prepare or just rush at it?
Refining ideas	Does s/he draft and edit ideas? Does the talk grow over time?
Note-making	Do notes cover keywords for the presentation? Are they too brief or too wordy?
Practice	Does she practise? How – by composing speech as writing? Practising to an audience? A mirror?

Points to watch for in content

Choice of item	Is it a suitable/interesting item? Is it a genuine choice or was it just handy?
Accuracy	Is the content factually accurate?
Effectiveness	Does s/he provide a bare minimum of detail, or
Keywords	Are the keywords good ones? Precise nouns, appropriate adjectives, powerful verbs?

GIVING THE TALK

Think about your audience – not yourself.

- Look at the audience. Talk directly to them. Give them a smile!
- When you are showing them something, make sure they can see it. Hold it up and point out special features as you describe them.
- Speak slowly and clearly so they can hear. Pause slightly between sentences.
- Speak up – don't mutter!
- Stand still and don't fidget.

If anything goes wrong, try to put it right without fuss.

Staging individual presentations

The logisitics of fitting 30-odd individual presentations into your classroom routine depend on individual circumstances. If possible aim for one or two half-hour sessions per day (for instance, at the beginning and/or end of the day). If children perform in groups of about six, it should be possible to get through the whole class's presentations in a week, devoting five to eight minutes to each child. If possible, ensure that the first couple of performers in each batch are fairly fluent readers and speakers. This allows less able pupils to familiarise themselves with the sentence frames and the sort of vocabulary and sentence patterns that are expected and appreciated.

You may wish to continue focused assessment of some pupils (see page 44), but during performances the teacher should be concentrating on modelling how to listen appreciatively and providing positive feedback. The sheet could be filled in immediately after the presentation, or completed during the presentation by another adult.

Points to watch for in language

Sentence structure	Does s/he use the frame to speak in sentences? Does expression indicate awareness of sentence boundaries? Are any extra sentences framed correctly?
Explicitness	Is the description clear, explicit, evocative? How much detail is there?
Vocabulary	Is vocabulary varied or repetitive? Has s/he used precise nouns, suitable adjectives and verbs?
Coherence	Are there many intrusive 'ands'? If the frame has been adjusted (e.g. singular to plural; *a* to *an*) is consistency maintained?
Standard English	Has s/he used the vocabulary and grammar of standard English?

Points to watch for in presentation

Pace	Is delivery too fast or too slow?
Voice	Is speech audible? Is the voice expressive or monotonous?
Audience engagement	Does s/he address the audience, maintaining eye contact?
Body language	Does s/he stand confidently or self-consciously? Does s/he make good use of any visual aids? Does s/he fidget?
Dealing with problems	Is s/he easily distracted? If anything goes wrong does s/he deal with it satisfactorily?

For many children, this may be the first time they have spoken in a non-interactive situation, and the experience may be quite worrying. After thanking each child for his/her contribution, give **at least one piece of positive feedback** such as:

- *I liked the way you used the frame/adjusted the frame to your needs.*
- *You really spoke with expression there – you sounded like a real expert!*
- *Your enthusiasm shone through – it made me want to rush off and find the book/programme/poem.*
- *I loved the way you gave that extra little bit of detail about . . .*

Be very careful in giving negative feedback, as too much criticism could put shy children off speaking up. Focus on the difficulties you had as a listener, rather than those of the pupil as a speaker, helping the child recognise what is important in being heard and understood:

- *Could you just say those first two sentences again – I didn't quite notice where the first one ended.*
- *Could you tell me more about . . . ? I can't imagine it yet.*
- *Could you say the last bit a little slower – I didn't quite catch it.*

If time allows, pupils could also be encouraged to answer questions from the audience about their item. This is much easier than a non-interactive speech.

■ Show and tell

A PERSONAL TREASURE

This is my _____ .

I have owned it for _____ *(how long?)* _____ .

I first got it _____ *(where?)*
_____ *(when?)* _____ .

It is special to me because _____
_____
_____ .

I keep it _____ *(where?)* _____
_____ .

'This is my **favourite scarf made from lovely soft wool called mohair that comes from a goat.**

I have owned it for **just over three years**.

I first got it **as a Christmas present from my gran**.

It is special to me because **I love the colour and it keeps me warm in the winter. Also, it reminds me of my gran, and she lives a long way away so I don't see her that often. I like to stroke it because it is so soft and comforting.**

I keep it **hanging on a hook on the back of my bedroom door, where I can see it when I go to sleep at night.**'

Talk about:

- Choosing a 'special treasure'. Give some examples to get them thinking, e.g.:

favourite toy	favourite clothes
holiday mementos	photographs
ornaments	Brownie or Cub badges

- The importance of detail to make the *Show and Tell* interesting (give an example of a monosyllabic performance, and explain that you want more). Tell children to imagine they're going on a TV show about favourite things, and want to impress the audience.
- Key questions a description such as this should answer: who, what, when, where, why, how?
- The changes necessary if the item is plural, e.g. beads, badges, playing cards. Use sticky notes to show changes:

  These are my .... I have owned them for ....
  I first got them .... They are special to me because ....
  I keep them ....

- changing *a* to *an* if the item begins with a vowel, e.g. ornament.
- using 'grown up language', such as *Also* instead of *And*
- building up the description as you plan your talk.

Use the sheet again...

...when studying characters in fiction. Ask pupils to take on the role of a character and think what would be their favourite treasure, e.g. Snow White's stepmother:

This is my **magic mirror that tells me I am the fairest of them all.**

I have owned it **for 20 years**.

I first got it **by poisoning its owner. She was a beautiful model and I couldn't bear her being more attractive than me.**

It is special to me because **it reminds me every day how lovely I am, and warns me if anyone else is getting above themselves and needs sorting out.**

I keep it **in my bedroom, where I can consult it first thing every morning and last thing at night.**

■ Show and tell

A NATURAL OBJECT

This is a _____ .

It is made of _____

_____ .

It is this shape because _____

_____ .

You might find one of these _____ *(where?)*

_____ because _____

_____ .

It is useful to humans because _____

_____

_____ .

'This is a **sunflower seed.**

It is made of **a hard stripy shell with a soft white seed inside**.

It is this shape because **it has to get buried in the soil to grow into a new flower. This small pointy shape can easily get pushed into the ground when people or animals walk by, or when someone ploughs the field.**

You might find one of these **in a garden or field** because **that is where sunflowers grow.**

It is useful to humans because **people and animals can eat them. Our parrot loves sunflower seeds and so do I. If the seed grows into a sunflower, it is beautiful to look at.'**

Talk about:

- What 'natural' means, and the difference between 'natural' and 'man-made' objects like tools.
- How natural objects are a particular shape, size, colour, texture for a reason.
- The importance of explaining clearly and 'stating the obvious'. Tell children to imagine they're a scientist from another planet who has to work out exactly why their chosen natural object is like it is, and why it is found in a particular place.
  possible items for pupils to talk about, e.g.:

leaves	seeds	flowers	snakeskin
cotton ball	twigs	vegetables	rocks
leather	honey	bird's nest	fruit
shells	sheep's wool	coal	peppercorns

  or any 'found' natural object. Tell them to talk about it with parents etc. to establish what it is made of, where it might be found and why.
- The changes necessary if the item is plural, e.g. seeds, leaves. Use postit notes to show the changes:

  These are .... They are made of .... They are this shape because .... You might find these .... They are useful to humans because ....

- Changing *a* to *an* if the item begins with a vowel, e.g. apple, onion.
- Using 'grown up language', such as *Also* instead of *And*.
- Building up the description as you plan your talk.

If a child is completely wrong, just say 'Gosh, that's interesting. I must check that up.' Return to the subject another time (after you've 'checked') and put the class right. This is less likely to inhibit the child from speaking out on future occasions.

■ Show and tell

A TOOL OR UTENSIL

This is a _____

_____ .

It is used for _____

_____ .

It is made of _____

_____ .

This is how it works – _____

_____ .

I chose to talk about a _____ because

_____ .

'This is a **pencil sharpener**.

It is used for **sharpening pencils when the lead gets too flat**.

It is made of **a plastic container, with a very sharp metal blade**.

This is how it works – **You put the blunt pencil in this hole here and turn it round. The sharp blade touches the wood of the pencil and shaves a strip off it. Gradually, it sharpens the pencil into a new point.**

I chose to talk about a **pencil sharpener** because **it's the sort of thing we use every day without thinking about it, but when you do think about it, it's a very clever invention**.'

Talk about:

- The meaning of 'tool or utensil'.
- What's important in a tool (e.g. size, shape, design, functionality) and what's not particularly important (e.g. colour, pattern).
- Thinking about how things work, and how to explain them.
- Being very explicit – not worrying about 'stating the obvious'. Tell children to imagine they're explaining their item to a Martian, who has no idea what it is or how it works. Choosing an item to talk about, e.g.:

toothbrush	bottle opener	elastic band	door catch
umbrella	scissors	sellotape dispenser	compass
tweezers	iron	paper clip	earring
hair clasp	zip	needle and thread	buckle
clasp of necklace	bottle top	knitting needles	stapler
key and lock	screwdriver	mousetrap	egg timer

  You could give a list, like a wedding present list, for pupils to choose from.
  Don't worry if several children choose the same item – the comparisons will be interesting.
- The importance of (a) choosing something simple (b) understanding **exactly** how it works before trying to explain it. The changes necessary if the item is plural, e.g. scissors, needle and thread. Use sticky notes to show the changes:

  These are .... They are used for .... They are made of ....
  This is how they work – .... I chose to talk about .... because ....

- Changing *a* to *an* if the item begins with a vowel, e.g. elastic band, umbrella.
- Using 'grown up' language constructions and vocabulary, such as *container*.
- Building up the description as you plan your talk.

Don't expect their explanations to be clear or even accurate at this stage!

■ My favourite

BOOK (FICTION)

My favourite book is _____

by _____ .

It is about _____

_____ .

My favourite character is called _____

_____ .

S/He is _____ .

I like this character because _____

_____ .

The part of the story I like best is when _____

_____ .

I would recommend this book to _____

because _____ .

'My favourite book is **Fantastic Mr Fox** by **Roald Dahl.**

It is about **a very clever fox who is hunted by three horrible farmers. The farmers try to dig him and his family out of their den, but they escape. Next they try to starve them out, but Mr Fox has a brilliant idea. In the end he saves his family and all the other digging animals, and the three farmers are left feeling miserable.**

My favourite character is **Mr Fox himself.**

He is **very cunning and clever, but also brave.**

I like this character because **even though he breaks the law, he is just doing it to save his family and he isn't as bad as the farmers, because they actually want to kill all the animals.**

The part of the story I like best is when **Mr Fox first thinks of a way to get some food. You can't imagine how he's going to do it, and then you realise what a great idea it is. I love it when he sends one of his children back with fat chickens for his wife, who is feeling very weak.**

I would recommend this book **to anyone – boys and girls –** because **it is very funny and exciting, and it is really easy to read. The author makes you want to keep turning the pages to find out what happens.**'

Talk about:

- the point of having a copy of the book as a 'visual aid' for your talk, and how it can be used;
- how to summarise a story in a few sentences, without spoiling it for others by giving away the ending or main surprises in the plot;
- the convention of 'S/He', and how to cross out the option that does not apply;
- how to explain and justify one's preference for a character or section of the story by thinking hard about what it is that appeals to you (always refer to the book for evidence) – see also Smorgasbord, page 82;
- what you have to think about in terms of recommending a book, e.g. gender, age, interests.

■ *My favourite*

TV PROGRAMME

My favourite TV programme is called _____ .

It is on _____ *(channel)* at _____ *(time)*

on _____ *(day of the week)* _____ .

It is about _____

_____ .

I like it because _____

_____ .

I would recommend this programme to _____

because _____ .

If you watch it, look out for _____ .

'My favourite TV programme is called **Coronation Street.** It is on **ITV** at **7.30 in the evening** on **Mondays, Wednesdays and Fridays – although sometimes the times change if there is football on.**

It is about **the people who live on a street in the north of England. There are lots of different families – some are nice and some are nasty. The street also has a corner shop, a cafe, a taxi firm and a pub called The Rovers Return.**

I like it because **I have watched it with my mum and dad ever since I was very little, so I know all the people really well. There are lots of exciting stories, but also lots of funny ones, and I like talking about it with my mum and my gran.**

I would recommend this programme to **all ages of people and both male and female** because **there is something for everyone. There are stories for old people and stories for young ones, and watching it brings the generations together.**

If you watch it, look out for **David Platt. He is a really evil character, and always up to no good. I like his sneaky smile when he's thinking up another of his schemes. My mum remembers when he was born, on Christmas Day!**'

■ *My favourite*

POEM (MODERN OR CLASSIC)

My favourite poem is a modern/classic poem called

_____ .

It is by _____ and it is about

_____ .

One of the ways you can tell it is modern/classic is

_____

_____ .

My favourite lines from the poem are:

_____

_____

_____ .

The reason I like these lines is that _____

_____ .

I also like _____:

_____

_____

because _____ .

'My favourite poem is a classic poem called **Escape at Bedtime.**

It is by **Robert Louis Stevenson** and it is about **a child who goes out into the garden at night to look at the stars. In the end the grownups chase him in and make him go to bed, but he still remembers the starry sky. It's also about the feelings you get when you look up at the night sky – it seems so enormous and exciting.**

One of the ways you can tell it is classic is **the old-fashioned language like 'parlour' (which is a room) and 'ne'er' (which means 'never'). But even though it was written a long time ago, the feelings it describes are the same as people have now.**

My favourite lines from the poem are:

> **The Dog and the Plough, and the Hunter, and all,**
> **And the star of the sailor and Mars,**
> **These shone in the sky, and the pail by the wall,**
> **Would be half full of water and stars.**

The reason I like these lines is that **I wanted to know what the Dog and the Plough and everything were, so my dad and I looked them up and went out to find them in the sky. I love the stories about the stars, and the way they have always been there to guide the sailors. The poem reminds me of my own feelings.**

I also like **the last line**:

> **But the glory kept shining and bright in my eyes,**
> **And the stars going round in my head.**

because **it makes me go all shivery. It is just like you feel when you have been watching stars**.'

Talk about:

- choosing a poem that will give you something to talk about (short humorous poems are not much use, because once you've said 'it's funny' that's it);
- being very familiar with the poem and learning your favourite section by heart;
- how to summarise a poem – it's very different from a book, and often there is no 'story', just a series of impressions;
- the sorts of clues that tell you roughly when the poem was written;
- thinking critically about why you like it.

Assessment sheet

Individual presentation

Name _____   Date _____

Preparation	Presentation
approach to planning	*use of speaking frame*
reflecting on content	*pace, volume, expression*
refining ideas	*engagement with audience*
note-making	*body language*
practice	*dealing with distractions/problems*
Content	**Language**
choice of topic	*sentence completion and coherence*
accuracy/research	*explicitness*
effectiveness	*vocabulary*
keywords	*standard English*

Suggestions for the types of behaviour to watch for are given on pages 28 and 30.

Group presentations

Group presentations provide opportunities for two sorts of talk:

- collaborative talk within the group around the specific task – talk for learning;
- participation in the formal presentation using the speaking frame – talk for writing.

Preparatory materials

Many thinking skills programmes are based on the first type of talk for learning: small group, open-ended discussion, in which pupils share and build on each other's ideas. The ideal size for a group seems to be between four and six.

However, for group discussion to be successful, the children need plenty of preliminary work to establish procedures and rules for behaviour. They should by now be familiar with speaking frames and how to use them, so the emphasis in the introduction to these activities is on developing (or revising) the ground rules of discussion. This discussion will involve making decisions about the specific content, and sharing out the sections for the eventual presentation.

The final formal presentation is a further opportunity to familiarise children with literate language patterns – this time language associated with instructions and processes. It also involves shared responsibility, formal turn-taking, and speaking in complete sentences. While the group provides support, each child has an individual responsibility for their part in the performance, e.g. speaking clearly, adopting an appropriate speed and volume.

Stage 1: How to...

The three activities are designed to develop clarity of thought about a variety of processes, and the language in which to explain these processes:

- **How to make ...**: defining the equipment required and the stages involved in a familiar process, and explaining them clearly and sequentially (scientific thinking).
- **Follow the rules**: defining the rules underlying familiar activities – sequential and non-sequential – and expressing these clearly (analytic thinking).
- **Use your imagination**: generating ideas for an imaginary process and explaining them in the terms already rehearsed above (creative thinking, analogy).

The frames specifically cover these aspects of literate talk:

- the imperative and/or second person instructions;
- sequential connectives (e.g. *When ...*) and sentence frames (*The first step ...*);
- causal connectives (e.g. *because; if ... , ...; so that*);
- conditional verbs for imagined events (*would*).

Stage 2: Four points

The activities are designed to provide opportunities for shared creative thinking, involving:

- generating and evaluating ideas;
- explaining and justifying ideas;
- discussing, arguing a case and reaching agreement.

The final presentation involves shared responsibility, formal turn-taking and speaking in complete sentences. While the group provides support, each child has an individual responsibility for their part in the performance, e.g. speaking clearly, adopting an appropriate speed and volume.

The frames specifically cover these aspects of literate talk:

- speaking in complete sentences, varying sentence construction;
- ways of introducing a number of non-sequential points *(Secondly, Another, A further, Finally)*;
- the 'tentative' language of creative thought *(could, would, possible, might be)*;
- varying expression *(One use would be; would be useful; could be used for)*;
- explanatory and justificatory language.

RULES FOR GROUP DISCUSSION

Listen to others:

- look at the speaker;
- try to remember what they say;
- ask questions if you don't understand;
- don't interrupt.

Make sure everyone gets a chance to speak:

- shy people – be brave!
- bold people – don't hog the floor!

Always be polite – especially when you disagree!

Give reasons for what you say, e.g.:

- 'I disagree because . . . '
- 'I think . . . because . . . '

There are no wrong answers – just steps towards a solution.

Take turns to be secretary and make notes.

Introducing group discussion

Before asking children to work in groups on a specific task, spend time establishing the ground rules for behaviour. Ideally, pupils should devise these for themselves through class discussion, thus ensuring they have ownership of – and therefore greater commitment to – the final list. However, through guiding discussion, ensure they cover all the points listed opposite (pages 80 and 82 might also be helpful).

When you have produced a list, put pupils into groups of about six to test them out on the following task:

- Each group member writes one rule on a strip of paper.
- Each group appoints one member to monitor the discussion.
- The remainder of the group then discusses the relative importance of each rule, and ranks them in order of importance.
- Groups feed back to the class on their final order, giving reasons for the ranking.
- Discussion monitors feed back on how well their groups abided by the rules, and make suggestions for further rules that might help.

If pupils are new to group work, they may find this activity taxing. Ensure you establish the rules firmly through class discussion, perhaps on several occasions, before trying again. Remember always to model the desired behaviour yourself during class discussion.

To introduce the activities:

- Display your *Rules for Group Discussion* and an enlarged copy of the relevant speaking frame.
- Read the frame with pupils. Discuss what is involved and how the group might organise itself to create the presentation.
- Give a small copy of the frame to each group.

You could use the assessment sheet on page 66 to focus on the work of one or two groups.

Points to watch for during preparation

Collaboration	Are they working as a team? How did they allocate/share tasks? Is anyone left out or too dominant?
Reflecting on content	Is there genuine discussion, reflecting on content?
Refining ideas	Are they building on each other's ideas, making improvements?
Note-making	Do notes cover keywords for the presentation? Is the secretarial system working? Is each child involved in making the notes for his/her section?
Practice	Do they use practice to improve content and presentation? Do they give useful feedback to each other?

Points to watch for in content

Choice of topic/ideas	How did they agree this? Is it suitable?
Accuracy	Are their instructions correct/appropriate/imaginatively acceptable?
Effectiveness	Do they organise ideas appropriately (e.g. lists, sequences?) and explain them clearly? In *Four Points* do they find arguments to justify their case?
Keywords	Are they choosing good keywords – precise nouns, necessary detail, verbs appropriate to the process?

GIVING THE TALK

1. Make sure you know who is going to say each section. Stand in the right order.

2. Don't waste time between speakers. Swap quickly, so the presentation flows smoothly.

3. When it's your turn:

    - look at the audience;
    - speak slowly, clearly and with expression;
    - don't fidget.

4. When it's not your turn, fade into the background:

    - look down, or at the speaker
    - don't make any sound
    - don't grin or giggle.

5. If anything goes wrong, work as a team to sort it out.

Staging group presentations

If children are working in groups of six, it should be possible to stage all the presentations in one session. Display an enlarged copy of the *Giving The Talk* notes opposite, and talk them through with pupils, reminding them about general points they have learned about speaking in public.

Start with an able group, so the less able children have the chance to see a model before performing themselves. Use your feedback to the early groups to help others – if early presentations do not work well, it might be helpful to discuss the problems, and give groups a little longer to prepare.

Points to watch for in language

Sentence structure	Does their delivery indicate awareness of sentence boundaries? Are any extra sentences framed correctly? In lists, are items clearly delineated?
Specific language features	Do instructions use procedural language (e.g. imperative verbs, sequential connectives) and does persuasion use the language of argument? Is the use of language consistent between speakers
Vocabulary	Is vocabulary varied or repetitive? Have they used precise nouns, suitable adjectives and verbs? Does their choice of connectives work?
Standard English	Have they used the vocabulary and grammar of standard English? Is there agreement in terms of tense, person, number?

Points to watch for in presentation

Turn-taking/ collaboration	Is their turn-taking organised or chaotic? Are they working as a group? Is their performance organised or chaotic?
Pace	Is the pace of the presentation/individual speakers satisfactory?
Voice	Is each speaker audible? Are voices expressive or monotonous?
Audience engagement	Do they address the audience or each other? Does their performance engage attention?
Body language	Does each speaker 'hold the floor' confidently? Do non-speakers fade back or attract attention?
Dealing with problems	Are they easily distracted? Do they work as a group to overcome problems?

At the end of each presentation, give brief feedback on key points of the performance, making praise specific wherever possible, e.g.:

- *I thought you were all very organised and used the different voices to make the instructions clear.*
- *I thought all your ideas were very interesting. I specially liked Mo's argument because she explained it very clearly.*
- *Your turn-taking was excellent, so the talk flowed smoothly with no disruption between speakers.*
- *I liked the way you enunciated your words so clearly, so we could hear every word.*

Where feedback is negative, give it from the point of view of the audience, e.g.:

- *It was hard to concentrate on what Ben was saying because people were moving behind him.*
- *I didn't always understand your points because the explanations were a bit muddled.*
- *I'm afraid you lost me a bit because of the big gaps when you swapped over.*

If you invite the rest of the class to comment on aspects of the performance (perhaps basing it on the *Giving The Talk* notes), ensure the criticism is constructive.

■ How to

MAKE...

Our group is going to explain how to make _____ .

| Before you start make sure you have _____ |
| _____ . |

| You will also need _____ |
| _____ . |

| Begin by _____ |
| _____ . |

| The next step is to _____ . |

For further steps choose from these connectives:

| When _____ , _____ . |

| After this, _____ . |

| Then _____ . |

| Now _____ . |

| While _____ . |

| Finally, _____ . |

'Our group is going to explain how to make **symmetrical butterfly pictures.**

Before you start, make sure you have **paintbrushes, a large piece of paper**, **some coloured felt pens and several colours of bright paint. The paint should be strong but quite runny.**

You will also need **newspapers or something to protect the surface you work on, and a sink for washing the paint pots afterwards.**

Begin by **folding the paper in half and opening it up again so you have a fold line going down the middle.**

The next step is to **paint half of a butterfly on one side of the fold line, with the body on the fold and the wing taking up most of the paper. Use lots of colours for the wing, and keep the paint quite runny.**

When **the half butterfly is done, fold the paper back over again, and press it down. Smooth your hand gently over it.**

Then **unfold the paper and you should have a symmetrical butterfly. It might be a bit blotchy, so wait for it to dry.**

Finally, **use your felt tips to tidy up the picture, by drawing a clear outline to the wings and body, adding antennae and so on.'**

Talk about:

- Choosing something for which pupils can create **sequenced** instructions addressed to only one person (e.g. most games involve several players, which causes compositional problems). Offer a variety of topics which the children should know about to each group, e.g.:

simple recipes, e.g.	**art activities**, e.g.	**class/school procedures**, e.g.
making a cup of tea	simple origami	making a computer printout
boiling an egg	wax relief painting	using a thesaurus
cheese on toast	pasta jewellery	getting a school dinner
scrambled egg	making 'playdough'	using the digital camera
making a sandwich	making a puppet	choosing/changing fonts.

  It does not matter if two groups choose the same topic.
- Listing ingredients (items you specifically need for this activity) and equipment (items you would generally use in this type of activity). Explain that pupils will probably think of more for each list as they discuss the process.
- Clarity in explaining the steps. This needs careful discussion, and plenty of thought about what is involved in each step. Children should not be afraid of 'stating the obvious'.
- Deciding on how many steps your activity takes, and selecting appropriate connectives (and rejecting others).
- Improving on your instructions as you practice.

■ How to

FOLLOW THE RULES

Our group has made a list of rules for
_____ .

These rules are important because _____
_____ .

The most important point to remember is _____
_____ .

Another key rule is _____
_____ .

For further steps choose from the sentence frames below:

If _____ , _____ .

_____ , so that _____ .

Always remember to _____ .

You should never _____ .

'Our group has made a list of rules for **getting your spelling correct when you are writing**.

These rules are important because **people judge you on your spelling, so you should try to get it right. You need to know how to do this on your own, without bothering the teacher, who is probably working with a group.**

The most important thing to remember is **when you are actually writing, you should not bother too much about spelling. You should be concentrating on what you are saying and how to say it. So when you are writing, 'have a go' at spelling. Come back and look at the spelling later – draw a pencil line under the words you think you've spelled wrong.**

Another key rule is **to always see if you can work out the right spelling yourself. Have a go on a bit of scrap paper. If you think you've got it right you can correct it.**

If **you can't work it out, try looking on the class list of common words, or typing it into the computer and using the spellchecker. You could also try asking a good speller, or even looking it up in the dictionary.**

You should never just think **'Oh, I can't be bothered' because when you find something out for yourself you are an independent learner. That is the best sort of learning.**

Talk about:

- Choosing some rules to list. Offer a variety of topics which the children should know about to each group, e.g.:

PE lessons	using items of school equipment	looking after a pet
art lessons	crossing a busy road	safe bicycling
using matches	the country code	school trips
classroom behaviour	playground behaviour	assembly

  It does not matter if two groups choose the same topic.
- The fact that rules are not necessarily sequential – how will they decide how to order them?
- Clarity in explaining the rules. This needs careful discussion, and plenty of thought about what is involved. Children should not be afraid of 'stating the obvious'.
- Deciding on how many rules an activity takes, selecting appropriate sentence frames, rejecting others and reordering if necessary. Pupils will almost certainly have to add in extra sentences – warn them to avoid too many *ands.* They should try to remember other connectives from previous frames.
- Improving on your rules as you practice.

■ How to

USE YOUR IMAGINATION

Our group has worked out a way to _____
_____ .

The first step would be to _____
_____ .

The next stage in the process would be to _____
_____ .

An important point would be _____
_____ .

For safety reasons it would be necessary to _____
_____ .

We think the best thing about our idea is _____
_____ .

To put this plan into operation you would need _____
_____ .

'Our group has worked out a way to **improve our school field.**

The first step would be to **dig up the grass from half of the field and put down wood chippings instead. Wood chippings are safer if you fall on them and do not get muddy like grass. When the grass is wet, children could still play on half of the field.**

The next stage in the process would be to **buy some good adventure playground equipment. We would like a big fortress, some ropes to swing on and a flying fox. We could also have a rope bridge and tunnels made of big pipes. There would also be a building that could be like a house, office, shop or hospital.**

An important point would be **to put this equipment in the best places on the field. Anything that people might fall off should be over the wood chippings.**

For safety reasons it would be necessary to **restrict the playground to older children. The little ones would have to have their own playground somewhere else.**

We think the best thing about our idea is **that we would have a great place to play at break and lunchtime. This would mean we would use up our extra energy and be better at working the rest of the day.**

To put this plan into operation you would need **a lot of money to pay for the wood chippings and play equipment and for the workmen to do all the work. You would also need to do it in the holidays when the children are not around.**'

Talk about:

- Choosing an idea to plan. Offer a variety of topics each group, e.g.:

improve the school	create a theme park
improve the classroom	organise a great school trip
improve the playground	throw a class party

  It does not matter if two groups choose the same topic.
- Using imagination, and allowing everyone to contribute.
- Clarity in explaining exactly what you mean. This needs careful discussion, and plenty of thought about what is involved. Children should not be afraid of 'stating the obvious'.
- Using the conditional verb form (*would be, would need*) to show that these are suggestions for an imaginary process.
- Selecting appropriate sentence frames, rejecting others and reordering if necessary. Pupils will almost certainly have to add in extra sentences – warn them to avoid too many *ands.* They should try to remember other connectives from previous frames.
- Improving on your ideas as you practise the presentation.

■ Four points

FOUR GOOD USES FOR A...

Our group has discussed and decided on four good uses for a _____ .

One use for this object would be as a _____ . This would be a good use because _____ .

Another possible use might be _____ , because _____ .

We also think it would be useful as _____ . Our reasons for thinking this are _____ .

Finally, it is _____ , so it could be used for _____ .

We think our best suggestion is _____ because _____ .

'Our group has discussed and decided on four good uses for a **jam jar.**

One use for this object would be as a **container for small objects like buttons, nails or paperclips.** This would be a good use because **the glass is transparent, so you could see immediately what you have got in there, and how many.**

Another possible use might be **as a home for small creatures like caterpillars or tadpoles, because you would be able to watch them through the glass, and they would also get plenty of sunlight. For caterpillars you would have to put a lid on so that they did not escape and holes in the lid so they could breathe.**

We also think it would be useful as **a vase for flowers.** Our reasons for thinking this are **that it is a waterproof container, so the flower water would not leak out, and that it is the right sort of size. You could decorate it by painting the outside in bright colours to match your room.**

Finally, it is **made of glass**, so it could be used for **lighting a fire, using the rays of the sun. If you were shipwrecked, you could make a pile of dry grass, then position the jar so the sun's rays were directed through it on to the grass. Eventually it would heat up enough to set them alight and you would have a bonfire to attract attention.**

We think our best suggestion is **the last one about using it to make a fire if you were shipwrecked** because **that is a matter of life and death.**'

Talk about:

● choosing an item to talk about – provide a selection of items and give one to each group, e.g.:

binbag	umbrella	scarf	pair of tights
matchbox	toilet-roll tube	pile of old newspapers	

● Thinking about and around the item; the group could brainstorm by first writing down at least one suggestion and then sharing ideas.
● Not being too quick to choose – the more you talk the better the ideas that develop.
● Ensuring that ideas are not too 'off the wall' – they should be reasonably practical.
● How to explain and justify the uses, using explicit organised sentences.
● The use of language in the frame to ensure that the four points are clearly delineated (state that there are four points at the outset; show clearly that you are moving from one point to the next, e.g. *One use ..., Another ..., We also think ..., Finally ...*)
● Note that language is varied (e.g. *One use would be; would be useful; could be used for*) – this is much more effective than repetitive enumeration, e.g. *The first use is; The second use is; The third use is...*
● The 'tentative' language of creative thought (*could, would, possible, might be*).

■ Four points

FOUR WAYS WE WOULD CHANGE...

Our group has decided on four ways we would change _____ .

The first change we would make would be _____ . This is a good idea because _____ .

Secondly, we would _____ .
We believe this would be an improvement because _____ .

A further improvement would be to _____ as this would _____ .

Finally, we would _____ . This would mean that _____ .

We think our best suggestion is _____ because _____ .

'Our group has decided on four ways we would change **the world.**

The first change we would make would be **to get all the money in the world and share it out so that everyone gets the same amount.** This is a good idea because **it would be fairer. There wouldn't be some very rich people and some people dying of starvation.**

Secondly, we would **make a law that everyone must be kind to animals.** We believe this would be an improvement because **animals deserve to be treated fairly just as much as humans.**

A further improvement would be to **stop people driving their cars so much**, as this would **help stop global warming, which would be good for the planet.**

Finally, we would **make sure that food was shared out fairly. The countries with lots of food would give some to the countries that don't have so much.** This would mean that **everyone would live comfortable lives.**

We think our best suggestion is **the first one about sharing the money equally**, because **as well as being fair, it would mean nobody was jealous of anyone else so there would be no stealing and no crime.'**

Talk about:

- Choosing an area for discussion – you could ask all groups to think generally about how they'd change the world, the law or children's rights, or to concentrate more specifically on areas close to home, e.g.:

  - school: rules, playground, uniform;
  - their environment: our town, our town centre, the local park;
  - leisure pursuits they know well: television, computer games, particular toys.

- Thinking about and around the item: the group could brainstorm by first writing down at least one suggestion and then sharing ideas.
- Not being too quick to choose – the more you talk the better the ideas that develop.
- How to explain and justify choices, using explicit organised sentences.
- The use of language in the frame to ensure that the four points are clearly delineated.

■ Four points

FOUR PEOPLE TO INVITE TO SCHOOL

The first person we would like to invite to school is
_____ because _____ .

Another person who deserves an invitation is
_____ . The reason we chose
him/her is that _____ .

The third person on our list is _____
because _____ .

Our final choice is _____, and our
reason is that _____ .

If we could only choose one person, it would be
_____ because _____ .

The main difficulty we had in choosing one guest
out of the four was that _____ .

'The first person we would like to invite to school is **Zac Efron** because **he is a brilliant actor and he could do a show for us and raise money for school funds.**

Another person who deserves an invitation is **Prince William.** The reason we chose him is that **lots of people in the school would like to meet him. Everyone has seen his picture so often that we feel as though we already know him.**

The third person on our list is **the Prime Minister** because **lots of us wanted to give him our opinions on important issues like fox hunting. We also thought he might be able to help us get a new swimming pool in town.**

Our final choice is **the Buddha**, and our reason is that **after finding out about him in RE, we admire him and would like to ask him questions.**

If we could only choose one person, it would be **Zac Efron** because **all the girls voted for him.**

The main difficulty we had in choosing one guest out of the four was that **they were all so different. We wanted them all to come for different reasons, so it was impossible to choose really.**'

Talk about:

- Choosing four people: each child in the group could choose one and pitch their case to the group, which then votes on the best four.
- Whether the four should be living or could you have choices from history too?
- The importance of having good reasons for your choices (give as many as possible for each choice – add extra sentences to the frame).
- How to explain and justify choices, using explicit organised sentences.
- The use of language in the frame to ensure that the four points are clearly delineated.
- The issue of gender: point out *him/her* and comment on *he/she* pronouns.

Assessment sheet

Group presentation

Group members _____

_____ Date _____

Preparation	Presentation
collaboration	*turn-taking and collaboration*
reflecting on content	*pace, volume, expression*
refining ideas	*engagement with audience*
note-making	*body language*
practice	*dealing with distractions/problems*
Content	**Language**
creativity	*sentence completion and organisation*
choice of ideas	*language of argument*
effectiveness	*vocabulary*
keywords	*standard English*

Suggestions for the types of behaviour to watch for are given on pages 49, 50 and 52.

Signpost smorgasbord

These frames introduce common 'literate language' constructions for expressing key ideas (and the interrelationships between ideas) which pupils will meet in literacy lessons and across the curriculum.

The frames familiarise children with literate language through the opportunity to 'play around' with useful constructions orally. As well as introducing these language patterns into their vocabulary (for both writing and speaking) the activities should develop general thinking and communication skills, as they deal with key expressions of ideas and relationships.

A lesson plan is provided for introducing each frame, although teachers may find that opportunities to use them crop up naturally in literacy lessons or other areas of the curriculum. Elements from the frames may also be used to create specific speaking frames for further paired, individual or group activities.

Illustrating punctuation

When using the speaking frames, ensure children are aware of punctuation (and its relationship to oral expression) by the use of visual symbols. Devise signals to represent commas and full stops, e.g.:

- comma – draw a large comma shape in the air with a finger;
- full stop – jab the air with a finger.

Always use these when demonstrating the frames and ask pupils to use them when feeding back to the class.

CAUSE AND EFFECT

When ...., _____

If ...., _____

................................, so _____

.... This causes _____

_____ because ....

The reason _____ is that........................

These frames introduce some common language constructions for explaining cause and effect. They are useful when children are preparing for explanatory writing in science, geography, etc..

Introductory lesson

- Introduce the terms *cause* and *effect* and ensure children know what they mean. Point out that in the frames:

  Cause = ... Effect = _____

- Illustrate by completing the first frame orally using a cause/effect that is either:

  - obvious (**When** the window is open, it is cold)
  - silly (**When** I eat peanuts, my hair turns purple)

  As you speak, indicate the point where the comma separates the two grammatical chunks by a visual symbol, e.g. drawing a large comma in the air with your finger.

- Ask pupils to fill the same cause and effect into the next three frames, indicating the comma in the same way, and a full stop with another symbol, e.g. jabbing the air with your finger.

  - **If** I eat peanuts, my hair turns purple.
  - I eat peanuts, **so** my hair turns purple.
  - I eat peanuts. **This causes** my hair to turn purple. (Note change in verb form).

- Point out that sometimes, as in the two constructions in the box, the effect is stated before the cause:

  - My hair turns purple **because** I eat peanuts.
  - **The reason** my hair turns purple **is that** I eat peanuts.

  (Note: Many children say 'The reason is because . . .' This is a tautology and frowned upon by sticklers for 'correct' English.)

- You may wish to point out that in the first two frames, the chunks can be reversed:

  - My hair turns purple **when** I eat peanuts.
  - My hair turns purple **if** I eat peanuts.

- Ask pupils in pairs to think up their own cause and effect and take turns to fit it into the frames (remind them of the verb change with *This causes*). Ask a number of pupils to feedback their results to the class, starting with more able pupils, so that the less able hear the model a few times before trying it themselves.

TIME CONNECTIVES

When................., ——————

After................., ——————

Since................., ——————

Before................., ——————

Until................., ——————

.... Then ——————

.... Next ——————

.... Later ——————

.... Afterwards, ——————

These frames introduce some common language constructions for expressing temporal relationships. This activity is useful as preparation for any type of chronological or sequential writing, such as story writing or cross-curricular recount, instructions or explanations.

Lesson plan

- Introduce the term *time connectives* and ensure children know what they mean. Point out that most of the frames are for expressing two chunks of information, related by time: .... and _____
- Illustrate by supplying a past tense event to be the first chunk each time and asking children to help you come up with a second chunk, e.g.:

  > **When** *Jack killed the giant, everyone cheered.*
  > **After** *Jack killed the giant, he went on TV.*
  > **Since** *Jack killed the giant, he has been a hero.*
  > **Before** *Jack killed the giant, he was just an ordinary boy.*
  > **Until** *Jack killed the giant, he was just an ordinary boy.*

  Indicate the point where the comma separates the two chunks by drawing the comma in the air with your finger. Don't try to analyse the time relationships* – it's better just to do examples.

- Some children find it helpful to see events marked along a timeline, so that the complexities of **before, until, after, since** are clarified visually. You could also try organising a human timeline, with children holding cards on which events are written.

Jack just an ordinary boy	→	Jack killed the giant	→	Everyone cheered	→	Jack went on TV

  — Jack a hero —

- Return to the frames and help children see how in every case you can swap the chunks around, e.g.:

  > *Everyone cheered* **when** *Jack killed the giant.*
  > *Jack became a hero* **after** *he killed the giant, etc.. (and no need for commas here!)*

- Show how the next four connectives come at (or near) the beginning of a new sentence and indicate a straightforward 'event → event'. Help children experiment:

  > *Jack killed the giant.* **Then/Next/Afterwards/Later** *he went on TV.*

- Ask pupils in pairs to do the same with another past tense event. More able children might be able to think of their own first chunk, but some will need ideas, e.g. *I came to school* or *Jack climbed the beanstalk*. Ask a number of pupils to feedback their results to the class, starting with more able pupils, so that the less able hear the model a few times before trying it themselves.

---

*When usually implies 'immediately afterwards' (and is also often causal).

After is very clearly sequential – two distinct events, one following the other.

Since (or **ever since**) either leads into a series of events (as in example above) or continuous state (e.g. *Since Jack killed the giant, I've been feeling sick*).

With **Before** and **Until** the earlier chunk comes second!

SEQUENCE OF EVENTS

First, _____   Second, _____   Finally, _____

First of all _____   Next _____

Eventually, _____

To start with _____   After that _____

At last, _____

To begin with _____   Then _____

At the end, _____

When _____ , _____.

This activity is useful preparation for chronological or sequential writing, such as story writing, or cross-curricular writing of recount, instruction or explanation text.

Introductory lesson

● Introduce the term *sequence of events* and ensure children know what it means. Point out that:

- the words in the first column are ways of starting a sequence;
- those in the second are for the middle of a sequence;
- the last column has words that can conclude a sequence.

Any word can be chosen from any column so there are many possible permutations, e.g.:

> *First...*   *After that...*   *In the end...*

However, certain forms of words are sometimes more appropriate than others, depending on the sentence.

● Illustrate writing a sequence of three events on the board, e.g. Morning school up to break time: *We take the register. We have a maths lesson. We go out for break.* Then select three suitable words or phrases from the lists and say the sentences with them in place:

> **First of all** *we do the register.* **Then** *we have a maths lesson.*
> **Finally***, we go out for break.*

Indicate any commas or full stops by drawing them in the air with your finger. Ask pupils to try alternative words and phrases, discussing whether they 'sound right'.

● Point out that, in sequences of more than three events, you can use extra connectives from the central column, avoiding repetition (one *Then* is fine; more than one sounds dreary). Add in another event:

> **First of all** *we do the register.* **Then** *we have a maths lesson.*
> **After that** *we have half an hour's reading.* **Finally***, we go out for break.*

● Demonstrate that the *When ..., ...* construction can be used anywhere (but preferably only once):

> **When** *school starts, we do the register.*
> **When** *that's complete, we have a maths lesson.*
> **When** *maths is over, we have half an hour's reading.*
> **When** *the bell goes, we go out for break.*

● Ask pupils in pairs to think up a simple sequence of events, e.g. things you do when you get up in the morning/when you get home from school/when you eat your packed lunch. Ask a number of pupils to feedback their results to the class, starting with more able pupils, so that the less able hear the model a few times before trying it themselves.

The frame can be used again, for oral or written work, whenever children are recounting sequences, e.g.:

● the events in a story, fable, legend, etc.;
● factual events such as a school outing, a historical story;
● sequential instructions or explanations.

ADDING INFORMATION

as well   too

Also ...

In addition, ...

What is more, ...

OPPOSING INFORMATION

but

However,

On the other hand, ...

Adding information

These frames introduce alternative ways of building up information. The natural way to do this in spontaneous speech is *and ... and ... and.* A wider vocabulary of connectives and sentence openings automatically improve children's writing and speech.

Introductory lesson

- Talk about how the word *and* is often overused. While it is fine to use it occasionally, written work can be much improved by learning and using a variety of connectives.
- Write up two facts which can be linked by *and,* e.g.:

    *Andy spent two weeks in Spain in May **and** he went to Devon for Christmas.*

    Ask pupils to demonstrate orally they can be linked using the other devices:

    *Andy spent two weeks in Spain in May. He went to Devon for Christmas **too**.*
    *Andy spent two weeks in Spain in May. He went to Devon for Christmas **as well.***
    *Andy spent two weeks in Spain in May. He **also** went to Devon for Christmas.*
    *Andy spent two weeks in Spain in May. **In addition,** he went to Devon ...*
    *Andy spent two weeks in Spain in May. **What is more**, he went to Devon ...*

- Ask children in pairs to do the same with another two facts linked by *and,* perhaps related to recent reading or cross-curricular work, e.g.:

    *Zeus was king of the Greek gods **and** he was god of thunder.*
    *A fable is a story with a moral **and** it is often about animals.*
    *Plants are useful to us as food **and** they make oxygen for us to breathe.*
    *Transport improved in Victorian times **and** there were many new inventions.*

- Ask children to feed back their sentences, joined in different ways. Ask which they like the best each time. Perhaps you could take a vote on it.

Opposing ideas

These frames introduce children to alternative ways of saying *but.* There is not a wide choice of suitable alternatives for this age group, but access even to a small variety of connectives can have a dramatic effect on children's writing and speech.

Introductory lesson

- Talk about the word *but* and how it introduces an opposite fact or point of view. In formal writing, *but* should never be used to start a sentence. Pupils therefore need an alternative to *but* for use in their writing and speech.
- Write up two facts which can be linked by *but,* e.g.:

    *Andy enjoyed Spain **but** he found Devon rather wet.*

    Ask pupils to demonstrate orally how to link the facts in other ways:

    *Andy enjoyed Spain. **However,** he found Devon rather wet.*
    *Andy enjoyed Spain. **On the other hand,** he found Devon rather wet.*

    Talk about how the use of *However* or *On the other hand* automatically makes the language sound more formal and grown up.

- Ask pupils in pairs to try linking the pairs of facts with each of the connectives:

    My friend likes reading. I prefer watching TV.

    As pairs report back, ask the class which versions they do/don't like, and why.

AT THE SAME TIME

As.............., ————————

While.............., ————————

Whilst.............., ————————

During.............., ————————

.... At the same time, ————————

.... Meanwhile, ————————

.... In the meantime, ————————

As well as connectives that show time passing, there are a group of connectives that indicate synchronicity. These can be useful in children's fiction writing and non-fiction recounts. None of these connectives were introduced in the Year 3 book.

Introductory lesson

- Display the speaking frames and ask whether children can explain how they are different from the time connectives studied previously. Establish that the time connectives on page 72 connect events that happened in sequence (before and after), whereas these connect events that happen at the same time.
- Provide an example by writing up two sentences, one of which sets the scene (straight line) while the other tells of another event that breaks into the scene (dotted line), e.g.:

    I was on my way to school. I spotted a sparrowhawk.

    and ask pupils to try them in the first four frames, e.g.:

    ***As** I was on my way to school, I spotted a sparrowhawk.*
    ***While** I was on my way to school, I spotted a sparrowhawk.*
    ***Whilst** I was on my way to school. I spotted a sparrowhawk.*
    ***During** my walk to school, I spotted a sparrowhawk.*

- Point out that:
    - you have to change the wording when you use ***During***
    - the ***While*** and ***Whilst*** sentences can be improved by removing *I was*
    - that another way of setting the scene is simply to say ***On my way to school**, I spotted a sparrowhawk.*
    - that in the first three sentences, you can reverse the order of the clauses, e.g. *I spotted a sparrowhawk **as** I was on my way to school.*

- The connectives in the box don't work with the above example. They are used when two events continue simultaneously (side by side), as opposed to one event breaking into another, e.g.:

    I was on my way to school. My mum was driving to work.

    Help children see that all the constructions work with this one.
- Ask pupils in pairs to think of two things that could happen at the same time, and try them in all the frames. During feedback, discuss whether all their constructions work, and if not, why.
- More able children may also enjoy learning the sentence connective ***Simultaneously***.

Note: ***When*** can also be used for simultaneous events (e.g. *When I was on my way to school, I saw a sparrowhawk*) but most children already know this. They would use the construction automatically, since ***when*** is almost always the conjunction of choice!

STATING A FACT

The fact is that ...

There is no doubt that ...

We know that ...

There is no question that ...

In fact, ...

There is evidence that ...

Most people agree that ...

probably

This activity is useful when talking about the difference between fact and fiction, but it also helps children establish the difference between fact and opinion (see next page).

Introductory lesson

- Introduce the term *fact* and discuss the difference between *fact* (non-fiction) and *stories* (fiction). Give some examples of each and ask pupils in pairs to produce more. Discuss their suggestions, and ask how we know whether something is a fact or not ('true or not true').
- Choose one of their facts to use with the frames, e.g.:

  > **The fact is that** it is Monday today.
  > **There is no doubt that** it is Monday today.
  > **We know that** it is Monday today.
  > **There is no question that** it is Monday today.
  > **In fact,** it is Monday today.

- Ask pupils in pairs to do the same with another incontrovertible fact, e.g. someone's hair colour (*The fact is that James is blond*). Ask a number of pupils to feedback to the class, so that they hear the constructions many times.
- If any children provide 'facts' about which there might be some doubt, refer them to the two sentence starts in the box, and demonstrate how these are used. If the issue doesn't arise naturally, point out the box and explain that sometimes we are not absolutely sure that something is a fact. On these occasions we need to be careful not to sound too sure. The two sentence starts are ways of doing this. Give examples and use the sentence starts with them, e.g.:

  > **There is evidence that** mobile phones are a health risk.
  > **Most people agree that** the world is getting hotter every year.
  > Seaside holidays are **probably** good for your health.

- Ensure children know that they should be very sure of themselves before they claim something is a fact.

STATING AN OPINION

I think …

I believe …

In my opinion, …

In my view …

My view is that …

It seems to me that …

I feel that …

When children are aware of the difference between *fact* and *fiction* they should also be introduced to the significance of *fact* versus *opinion.* This in turn leads to ways of justifying opinion (see next page).

Introductory lesson

- Introduce the term *opinion* and discuss the difference between a fact (which everyone agrees is true) and an opinion (about which there could be disagreement). Give some examples of opinions (e.g. *It's too hot today. Dogs are better pets than cats*) and ask pupils in pairs to think of more.
- Choose one of their opinions to use with the frames, e.g.:

    I think *it is too hot today.*
    I believe *it is too hot today.*
    In my opinion, *it is too hot today.*
    In my view, *it is too hot today.*
    It seems to me that *it is too hot today.*
    I feel that *it is too hot today.*

- Ask pupils in pairs to do the same with another opinion. Ask a number of pupils to feedback to the class, so that they hear the constructions many times.

> This set of frames can be revisited whenever children are giving opinions on aspects of their reading. It should be used alongside the next set ('Justifying an opinion').

JUSTIFYING AN OPINION

My reasons for thinking this are _____

_____ .

I think this because _____ .

I have _____ reasons for this opinion.
They are _____ .

The justification for my point of view is that _____

_____ .

Children are frequently asked to give opinions throughout the curriculum. This set of frames helps with the general expression of the reasons behind one's personal preferences. The frames on the next page relate specifically to textual evidence.

Introductory lesson

- Introduce the term *justify* ('give good reasons for') and talk about why it is important to be able to justify our opinions – we should always think carefully about what we say and why we think it; thoughtlessness can lead to prejudice and problems.
- Demonstrate by providing an opinion, e.g. *In my opinion, EastEnders is the best TV soap.* Illustrate how to use the first frame to justify the opinion, e.g.:

   My reasons for thinking this are *that there are lots of good storylines and it is really true-to-life.*

- Ask pupils to express the same justification using the remaining frames.

   I think this because *there are lots of good storylines and it is really true-to-life.*
   I have two reasons for this opinion. They are *that there are lots of good storylines and it is really true-to-life.*
   The justification for this point of view is *that there are lots of good storylines and it is really true-to-life.*

- Ask pupils in pairs to discuss their opinions on issues relevant to them, e.g. *school uniform; homework; the length of school holidays; favourite TV programmes.* Ask for statements of opinion (children could select different ways of expressing these using the frames on page 80).
- For each statement, ask pupils to provide justification using one of the frames. Ensure they hear each of the frames used a number of times.

GIVING EVIDENCE

_____ . The evidence is …

_____ . The proof of this is …

_____ . We know this because …

_____ . This is shown on page …, where the writer says …

_____ .The words that tell us this are …

On page …, the author says … This suggests that
_____ .

indicates	implies	shows

Use these frames to introduce the idea of evidence, especially in reading, and to help children justify their inferences. Critical reading – 'interrogating the text' – is a good preparation for critical thinking in general and thus intellectual good health. All children are capable of critical thought, but articulating reasons for opinions and impressions is not easy, so the more help we can give the better.

Introductory lesson

- Introduce the term *evidence* (proof) and talk about why it is important to provide evidence for our impressions. Refer back to previous work on justifying opinions and explain that, when talking about books, the justification comes from the text. We should be able to find our evidence and help other people to see it.
- Use an example of inference from your current reading and provide the evidence. Ask children to use each of the speaking frames to express it.
- Set another question relating to current reading (or a number of questions for different groups) and ask pupils to discuss in pairs, find the evidence, and express it using each of the frames. In feedback, ensure they hear each of the frames several times.

> This set of frames can be used frequently during shared and guided reading to help children formulate and articulate the reasons behind their responses to text.

COMPARISON

_____ and _____ are both ...

_____ and _____ are alike in that ...

_____ and _____ are similar because ...

_____ and _____ have the following points in common: ...

One similarity between _____ and _____ is that ...

Another ...

A further ...

These frames are useful in many contexts, e.g. comparing characters or settings in literacy lessons; comparisons in cross-curricular writing, especially non-chronological reports.

Introductory lesson

- Introduce the terms *compare* and *comparison* and ensure children know what they mean (looking for ways in which things are the same).
- Explain that in spontaneous speech most children would say something like '_____ and _____ are the same because ...'. This is a rather ugly construction, and not exactly accurate (unless the two items are exactly the same in all respects).
- Illustrate by choosing two items to compare, e.g. a chair and a pencil. This is a useful open-ended thinking skills activity, because one can usually think of some points of comparison between even the most disparate objects. Elicit some points and ask pupils to feed them into each of the frames, e.g.:

    A chair and a pencil are both solid.
    A chair and a pencil are alike in that they are found in classrooms.
    A chair and a pencil are similar because both are man-made.
    A chair and a pencil have the following points in common: they are both solid, man-made and found in classrooms.
    One similarity between a chair and a pencil is that they can both be made of wood.

    Point out that the final frame can be converted (by the substitution of *A further* or *Another*) to be used when additional comparisons are given.
- Ask pupils in pairs to think of two objects and find enough points of comparison to fill all the frames. If possible they could fill in *Another similarity* and *A further similarity*. Ask pairs to feed their comparisons back to the class so that all pupils hear the various ways of comparing information many times.

CONTRASTING

_____ and _____ are different in that ...

A major difference between _____ and _____ is that ...

_____ and _____ differ in that ....

_____ is .... but _____ is ....

_____ is .... while _____ is ....

_____ is .... whereas _____ is ....

Some ways in which _____ and _____ differ are ....

These frames are useful in many contexts, e.g. contrasting characters or settings in literacy lessons, or contrasts in cross-curricular writing, especially non-chronological reports.

Introductory lesson

- Introduce the terms *contrast* (same word used for verb and noun, though a different pronunciation for each) and ensure children know what it means (ways in which things are different).
- Explain that in spontaneous speech most children would say something like '_____ and _____ are different because ...' but there are lots of other ways of expressing it, to help you vary your use of language.
- Illustrate by choosing two items to contrast, e.g. a chair and a pencil. Elicit some points of difference and ask pupils to feed them into each of the frames, e.g.:

    A chair and a pencil **are different in that** the chair is much bigger.
    A major difference between a chair and a pencil is that you cannot use a chair to write with.
    A chair and a pencil **differ in that** chairs are comfortable to sit on, **but** pencils are not.
    A chair is often made of metal **but** a pencil is always made of wood.
    A chair is quite expensive to buy **while** a pencil is cheap.
    A chair is usually too heavy to carry around **whereas** a pencil is portable.
    Some ways in which chairs and pencils differ are that they are different in size and cost, pencils are to write with while chairs are to sit on, pencils are more portable than chairs, and chairs may be made of metal, while pencils aren't.

- Draw attention to the use of the same conjunctions as we met in *Opposing information* (*but, while*) with the addition of another (*whereas*). Indeed, the whole point of contrast is to draw attention to opposing points.
- Ask pupils in pairs to think of two objects and find enough points of contrast to fill all the frames. Ask pairs to feed their comparisons back to the class so that all pupils hear the various ways of comparing information many times.

Appendix: Learning, language and literacy across the curriculum

The following edited extracts from *How to Teach Writing Across the Curriculum: Ages 8–14* explain the 'two horses' model of teaching more fully, showing how speaking frames fit into the overall framework. For more detail, case studies and teaching materials, see *How to Teach Writing Across the Curriculum: Ages 8–14*.

The two horses model for cross-curricular literacy

You can't teach children to write before they can talk. It's putting the cart before the horse.

It's over a decade now since a teacher in Yorkshire uttered those words at one of my inservice courses. As I drove home that night I started wondering exactly how teachers could ensure that the 'horse' of talk was properly hitched up to draw the 'cart' of writing.

Eventually, after long conversations with many colleagues I concluded that, in order to write, students need two sorts of talk:

- talk for learning – plenty of opportunities to use the simple spontaneous language of speech to ensure they understand the ideas and content they're going to write about;
- talk for writing – opportunities to meet and internalise the relevant patterns of 'literate language', to help them turn that content into well-crafted sentences.

So students need not one but two 'horses' to draw the writing 'cart'.

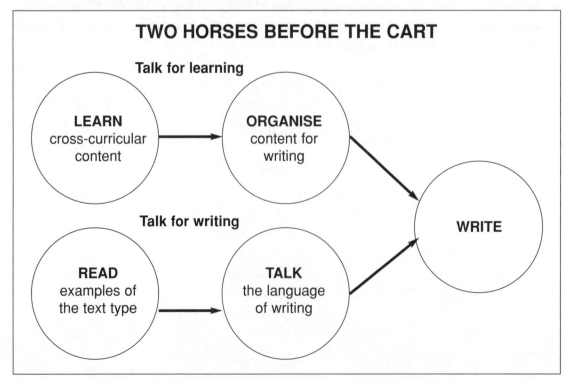

TWO HORSES BEFORE THE CART

Talk for learning

LEARN cross-curricular content

ORGANISE content for writing

Talk for writing

READ examples of the text type

TALK the language of writing

WRITE

Figure 4 Two horses before the cart basic model

Talk for learning

Learn cross-curricular content

In order to understand the content of cross-curricular teaching, apprentice writers need – just as they have always needed – plenty of opportunities for talk. These are provided through the sort of 'active learning' that provides opportunities for speaking and listening, such as:

- opportunities for imaginative engagement – drama, role-play, 'hot-seating';
- outings, excursions, field trips and other opportunities to find out about the wider world through experience and talk to a range of adults;
- active engagement in learning whenever possible – experimenting, making pictures, models, collages, websites, 'TV documentaries' etc. (there are now so many ways of creating audio and video records of learning activities);
- audio-visual aids for learning – for instance, relevant items to look at, touch and talk about;
- storytelling – listening to adults telling stories and anecdotes, and having opportunities to tell them themselves;
- responding to ideas through music, movement, art and craft.

Of course, in addition, students need opportunities to talk about and around ideas, through frequent opportunities for paired talk, and group or class discussion.

Such opportunities for active, motivating learning should be provided in all areas of the curriculum, whether by subject specialists in secondary school or by the class teacher in top primary. With so much attention these days to 'pencil and paper' work, it is sometimes tempting to think that they're a waste of valuable time. In fact, they're essential not only for learning, but for language and literacy development – and they're the obvious way to make the best use of cross-curricular links to literacy.

Organise content for learning

The different text types are characterised by their underlying structures – the ways that particular types of information are organised for writing. Awareness of these structures can become a powerful aid to understanding, allowing students to organise their learning in the form of notes or pictures before – or **instead of** – writing.

Skeletons for writing

I originally devised the 'skeleton' frameworks shown in the box for the English National Literacy Strategy. At the time, we called them 'graphic organisers' or 'diagrammatic representations', neither of which was a snappy title to use with primary children. It was a boy in the north east of England who christened them. He rushed up to his teacher with the words: 'They're skeletons, aren't they, Miss? They're the skeletons that you hang the writing on!' Thanks to that unknown Geordie lad, the skeleton frameworks became instantly memorable.

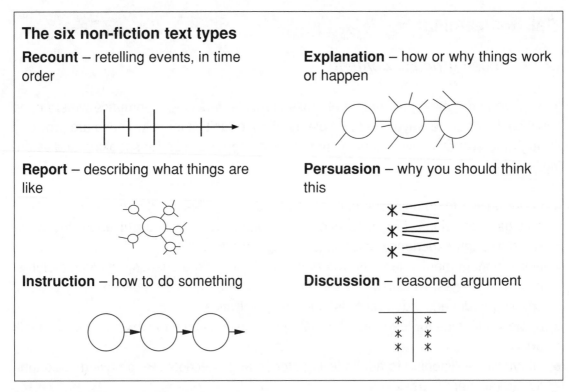

The six non-fiction text types

Recount – retelling events, in time order

Explanation – how or why things work or happen

Report – describing what things are like

Persuasion – why you should think this

Instruction – how to do something

Discussion – reasoned argument

Figure 5 A range of skeletons

How to use skeletons

Skeleton planning provides a link between cross-curricular content and specific teaching of writing skills. All teachers (whether or not they're responsible for literacy teaching) can introduce students to these ways of organising ideas by:

● demonstrating how to use skeletons themselves as simple note-taking devices and aide-memoires throughout the curriculum;
● teaching students how to draw the skeletons, and recognise which sorts of ideas and texts are associated with each skeleton;
● sending skeleton notes to the literacy lesson, so they can be used to link knowledge and understanding acquired in a wide range of subject areas with the literacy skills required to record that understanding.

Debbie Billard, a teacher in Rotherham, coined the term 'memory-joggers' for the jottings on a skeleton framework. She explains that memory-joggers are not proper sentences, nor do they have to be words at all. Notes, diagrams, symbols, pictures, photographs are all acceptable – anything that will jog the memory when one comes to write.

The skeleton can then be used like a carrier bag to bring this cross-curricular content to the literacy or English lesson. Once students have been taught the relevant language features of recount text, they can use their memory-joggers to write. Debbie's suggestion is to 'turn your memory-joggers into sentences'.

Teachers who have used skeleton frameworks with their classes have pointed out a number of advantages:

- making skeleton notes helps students organise what they have learned to aid memorisation of the facts;
- many students (especially boys) find it helpful to make this kind of 'big picture' record, so they have an overview of the whole piece of writing before beginning to write (which is, by its nature, a linear sequential process, rather than a holistic one);
- today's students are highly visually literate and skeleton planning helps them use visual memory skills to aid learning;
- as students learn a repertoire of skeletons, they can use them to take notes for a variety of purposes, not just as a precursor to writing;
- skeletons allow teachers and students to make clear links between literacy skills and the rest of the curriculum;
- planning on a skeleton allows students to organise the content of their writing in advance (including dividing material into sections and paragraphing) – it means that when they actually settle down to write, they can concentrate entirely on the language of writing;
- making a skeleton with the class provides an opportunity for highly focused speaking and listening;
- making a skeleton with a partner is an excellent focus for paired talk;
- using skeletons develops students' thinking skills.

It seems clear from talking to teachers that skeletons have the potential to be more than simple planning devices for writing. Perhaps the most exciting suggestion is that skeleton planning can become a way of developing generic thinking skills – helping students recognise the different ways human beings organise their ideas, depending on the subject matter we're addressing.

Talk for writing

Once students securely understand the content they are to write about, they need help in acquiring appropriate language structures to express it. Each of the text types is characterised by certain language features. The teaching of cross-curricular writing therefore provides many opportunities for revisiting aspects of grammar within a purposeful writing context.

However, care should always be taken not to *over-focus* on grammatical or stylistic elements at the expense of meaning. This is why 'word' and 'sentence' level teaching are best covered separately from meaningful writing tasks. 'Shared Writing' then provides an opportunity to illustrate how these elements are used in writing, referring to them briefly and tangentially without interfering with the overall flow.

It's also important that students' own assessment of their work should not be a mere exercise in box ticking against a checklist of language features. When teaching focuses on the bureaucracy of learning at the expense of the meaningful whole, there's a price to pay in students' motivation, understanding and – in the long run – ability to write (and think) well and fluently.

Read examples of the text type

Reading, in any aspect of literacy, should always precede writing. Every teacher knows that students who read lots of fiction for pleasure tend also to be good at writing fiction

– they absorb the rhythms and patterns of narrative language through repeated exposure. They also pick up new vocabulary by meeting it in context. Nowadays however, with the ready availability of screen based entertainment, fewer students see the point of reading for pleasure, so fewer of them tend to be 'natural' storytellers.

This has, in fact, always been the case with non-fiction writing. The non-fiction text types described in the previous section have various textual characteristics with which writers need to be familiar, but only the most voracious readers of non-fiction are likely to be familiar with them (and then, usually, only in limited genres).

Reading aloud

The most obvious way to expose all students to literate language patterns is to read well written non-fiction aloud – magazine and blog articles, short sections from textbooks, and so on. This helps familiarise them – via their ears – with the vocabulary and language patterns of the text types. As Robert Louis Stevenson put it, this is an excellent way of sensitising young minds to '*the chime of fine words and the march of the stately period*'.

Another excellent strategy is to provide opportunities for students to read non-fiction texts aloud themselves. This gives them the chance to hear literate language patterns produced from their own mouths; to know how standard English and sophisticated vocabulary *feels*; to respond physically to the ebb and flow of well-constructed sentences, learning incidentally how punctuation guides meaning and expression. There's a pay off in both speech and writing when we let accomplished authors put words into our students' mouths.

Reading aloud has acquired a bad reputation in recent years. The traditional technique of 'reading round the class' is embarrassing for poor readers and excruciatingly boring for good ones. But there are other ways of giving students opportunities to read decent texts aloud.

One is **paired reading**, when two students share a book or short text, dividing the reading between them. Depending on their level of ability, this could be alternate pages or alternate paragraphs. (For special needs students, reading alternate sentences encourages them to look for the full stops, and thus take note of sentence boundaries.)

When the class needs some subject knowledge, paired reading of a text is a good way to provide it.

Another is **reader's theatre**, when a group of students are asked to prepare an oral presentation of a short text for the rest of the class. There's no room here to describe it at length, but you'll find plenty of details and good ideas on the internet.

Talk the language of writing

Speaking frames

We can also provide opportunities for students to innovate on written language patterns by creating speaking frames for the sorts of vocabulary and sentence structures we want them to produce in their writing.

Sentence level work

In terms of teaching text types, sentence level teaching should be very light-touch, and – as far as possible – should engage students in active investigation of language.

This usually begins with **shared reading** of examples of a particular text type and talk about how authors express their ideas. Students can then be sent off to collect examples of the sorts of language they use from other similar texts, e.g.

- time connectives in recount;
- imperative verbs in instructions;
- the use of examples in report;
- causal language structures in explanation;
- the language of generalisation in persuasion;
- ways of clearly stating opposing views in discussion.

Students can be alerted to grammatical patterns through

- oral games, e.g. changing verbs into the past tense;
- class collections of words and phrases (e.g. posters for time connectives, ways of conveying cause and effect words; banks of useful adjectives, etc.);
- focused speaking and listening activities in which students create sentences of their own, featuring the appropriate language features (e.g. 'Speaking Frames').

The key to all these activities is plenty of opportunity to be actively engaged, especially in speaking and listening. Sometimes it's possible to do this as a class, but more often the solution is paired work.

Paired work

Each pupil is allocated a 'talking partner' – someone with whom they can be trusted to work well. Whenever the opportunity arises you say: 'Turn to your partner. You have 30 seconds [or two minutes, or whatever] to discuss . . .' Selected pairs can then retell their deliberations to the class.

Teachers who have used this system effectively stress the importance of training and careful organization in the early stages.

- One student can work as the teacher's partner to model the appropriate behaviour, then the class splits into pairs to try it. There should also be opportunities to discuss the point of the exercise, and good and bad points of procedure.
- Snippets training videos can also be useful for showing the class how the system works.

However, once the system is up and running, it can become a regular part of classroom life. Robin Alexander's book *Dialogic Teaching* illustrates how throwing ideas to students for discussion in pairs provides far greater opportunities for them to engage with ideas, to use technical vocabulary, and thus to internalize learning.

For special needs students, talking partners can also double as 'writing partners', allowing them to take advantage of oral rehearsal and oral revision of their work.

Our 'two horses' model for cross-curricular writing now looks like this:

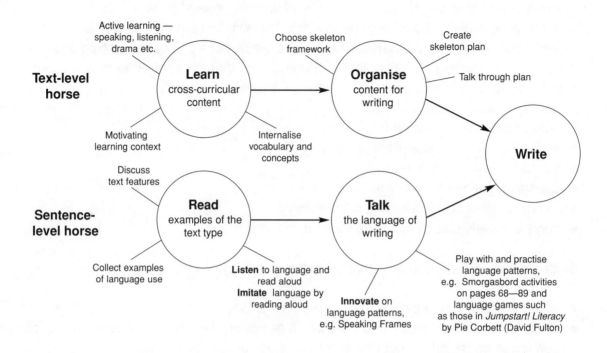

Figure 6 Two horses before the cart model

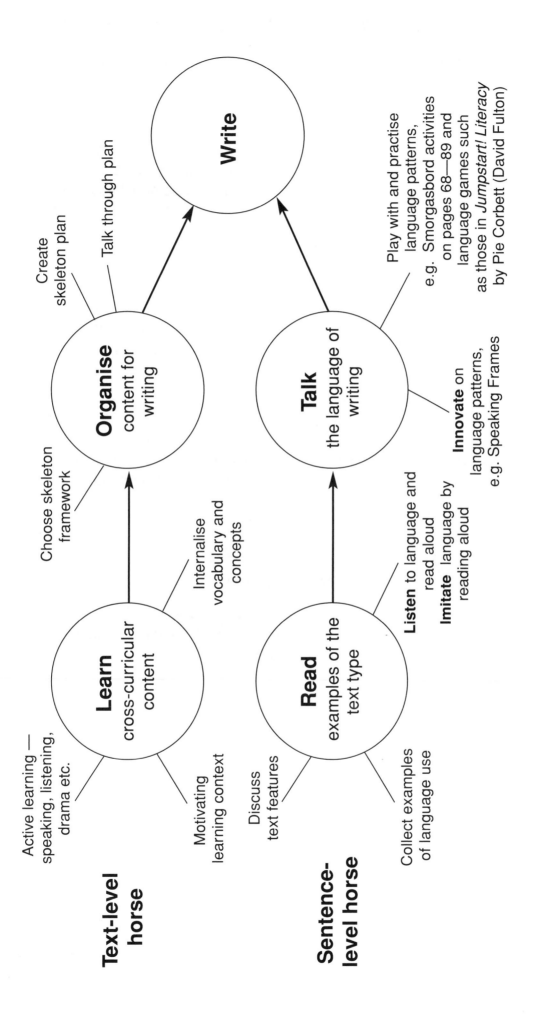

Text-level horse

Sentence-level horse

Write

Create skeleton plan

Talk through plan

Organise content for writing

Choose skeleton framework

Internalise vocabulary and concepts

Learn cross-curricular content

Active learning — speaking, listening, drama etc.

Motivating learning context

Discuss text features

Talk the language of writing

Play with and practise language patterns, e.g. Smorgasbord activities on pages 68—89 and language games such as those in *Jumpstart! Literacy* by Pie Corbett (David Fulton)

Innovate on language patterns, e.g. Speaking Frames

Listen to language and read aloud

Imitate language by reading aloud

Read examples of the text type

Collect examples of language use

The six non-fiction text types
and their application across the curriculum

Recount

retelling events in time order

accounts of schoolwork/outings
stories from history or RE
anecdotes and personal accounts
biographical writing in any subject

Report

describing what something is (or was) like

aspects of life in a historical period
characteristics of plants/animals
descriptions of localities/geographical features

Explanation

explaining how/why something happens

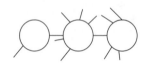

why historical events happened
how things work/come about in science,
   geography, etc.

Instruction

telling how to do or make something

art, DT, PE activities
procedures in maths/ICT/science
class or school rules

Persuasion

arguing a case; trying to influence opinion

'publicity campaigns' (articles, posters, leaflets)
   in any subject
expressing viewpoints on controversial topics in
   any subject

Discussion

a balanced argument

stating the case on both sides of a controversy
   in any subject
writing objective 'essays'

The key ingredients of non-fiction text types

	Recount	Report	Explanation	Instruction	Persuasion	Discussion
Audience	Someone who is interested in what happened	Someone who wants to know about something	Someone who wants to understand a process	Someone who wants to know how to do something	Someone you are trying to influence	Someone who is interested in an issue
Purpose	To tell the reader what happened in an informative and entertaining way	To present information so that it is easy to find and understand	To help someone understand a process	To tell someone how to do something clearly	To promote a particular view in order to influence what people do or think	To help someone understand the issue
Examples	• autobiography • newspaper article • history book	• dictionary • reference book • text books	• car manual • encyclopaedia • science text book	• recipe • instruction manual	• adverts • fliers • newspaper editorial	• news feature • essay on causes of something e.g. global warming
Typical structure	• paragraphs organised in chronological order	• paragraphs – not in chronological order • often organised in categories with headings/sub-headings	• series of logical steps explaining how or why something occurs	• chronological order • often in list form • diagrams, visual	• often a series of points supporting one viewpoint • logical order	• paragraphs • often a series of contrasting points • logical order
Typical language features	• past tense • first or third person • time connectives	• formal and impersonal • technical vocabulary • present tense • generalises • detail where necessary	• casual connectives • technical vocabulary • formal and impersonal • present tense	• simple and clear formal English • imperative • numbers or time connectives	• emotive language • personal language • weasel phrases	• present tense • formal and impersonal • logical connectives

With thanks to Julia Strong of the National Literacy Trust

David Fulton Books

Second Editions

How to Teach Writing Across the Curriculum

Sue Palmer

Series: Writers' Workshop

Now in updated second editions, *How to Teach Writing Across the Curriculum: Ages 6–8* and *8–14* provides a range of practical suggestions for teaching non-fiction writing skills and linking them to children's learning across the curriculum. With new hints and tips for teachers and suggestions for reflective practice, these books will equip teachers with all the skills and materials needed to create enthusiastic non-fiction writers in their classroom.

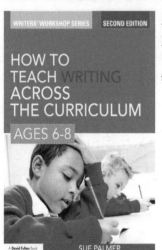

Ages 6–8

August 2010: A4: 112pp
Pb: 978-0-415-57990-2:
£19.99

Includes:

- techniques for using speaking and listening, drama and games to prepare for writing
- suggestions for the use of cross-curricular learning as a basis for writing
- planning frameworks and 'skeletons' for children to use
- information on key language features of non-fiction texts
- examples of non-fiction writing
- guidance on the process of creating writing from note-making.

New Material: More emphasis on creativity and the creative process – giving teachers more suggestions for working with the freed up curriculum. New pedagogical features with teacher 'hints and tips' have been added throughout.

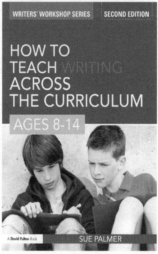

Ages 8–14

August 2010: A4: 112pp
Pb: 978-0-415-57991-9:
£19.99

Includes:

- information on the organisation and language features of the six main non-fiction text types
- suggestions for the use of cross-curricular learning as a basis for writing
- planning frameworks for children to use
- advice on developing children's writing to help with organisational issues
- examples of non-fiction writing
- suggestions for talk for learning and talk for writing
- information on the transition from primary to secondary school.

New Material: The two horses teaching model is introduced with extended material on speaking and listening. There is additional material on transitions and the early secondary level and photocopiable resources for teachers and recommended resources have been updated.

Routledge
Taylor & Francis Group

www.routledge.com/teachers